THE BIGGS TIME

THE BIGGS TIME

Michael Biggs
with Neil Silver

First published in 2002 by

Virgin Books
Thames Wharf Studios
Rainville Rd
London W6 9HA

ISBN 1 85227 988 5

Typesetting by Phoenix Photosetting, Chatham, Kent

Printed and bound by
Mackays of Chatham

ACKNOWLEDGMENTS

I would like to thank: Neil Silver for his help with preparation of the manuscript, Ode', Marcos de Oya & family, John & Lia Pickston, Paulo Garcia, Charmian Brent, D. Dulce & family, Fred Sill, Woody & family, the Deffenses, Brian Running, Dennis & Maura, the late Gus & Sheila, Chico Chagas, Pedro Barreto, Wellington Ivan Dias, Guga Murray, Lauro Benevides, Kevin Crace, Richard & Sharon Mallett, Kirsty Porter, Gio & family, George and all from the Tardis crew, Nick & Bruce Reynolds, Judy Totton, Roy Shaw, Roy Pickard, Chris Pickard, Rosa & family, Dickye, D. Shabbs & Sef, J. Cahill, Jane & Steve Wearing, Ray & Pixie, Mum, Alex & Celia, Uri Geller, Steven Berkoff, Mike Gray & family, Jacques Rene, Angina Joshi, Nigel Sangster, Activ-8.com, Harry Cohen M.P., Sotiris, D. Irene & Marcelo, Kevin Rawlings, Spider, Helga, The Crockers, Xara & family, Max, Jim, Valmir, Eric & Angela, The Foremans, Trevor Haylett, the Virgin crew, Sergio Granha, Die Toten Hosen, Ian, Blitz, Sta. Tereza, Barnet, Botafogo & Arsenal F.C., and to David Blunkett and the Home Office for my UK passport!

And all the ones who of course wish to remain anonymous.

CONTENTS

PROLOGUE 'ARE YOU RONALD ARTHUR BIGGS?'

The team from the *Sun* put their plan into action, organising a plane to take us back to England, and a passport in the name of Ronnie Biggs – his first since he'd fled England under a false passport back in 1965. I was concerned about how it was all going to turn out, and when the *Sun* had advanced us enough money to cover our debts, I said to Dad, 'Let's fuck 'em Dad, we don't have to go through with this. We've cleared our debts, we can go home. We can then even sell our story to another paper, how we screwed the *Sun*.' That was when my dad looked me in the eyes and wrote on the pad he'd used to communicate with me since his second stroke, 'Michael, you don't understand, I *want* to go home. I don't want to be the lonely, sick train robber left in Brazil, condemned to thirty years, living the rest of my life in exile. I want to fight them. If I die I want to die fighting, with dignity.' At that moment I realised, he's got a point, he's right. This is not about screwing the *Sun*, it's about his life, about closing a chapter. This is when it all finally sank in; my dad who had lived on the run for so many years – all my life – was going to return to Britain.

He had his reasons for wanting to go home and it was time to go, the opportunity provided by the journalists shadowing us with the three things he had demanded – a new suitcase, a portable CD player so that he could listen to his favourite jazz music, and a haircut.

When I look back, it was funny to think that all these rival journalists were running around Rio trying to find out where Ronnie Biggs was, when in fact he was holed up not too far from his own house in a mansion belonging to an American friend. The hunt for my dad was led by TV Globo, the main station; little did they know that Ron was tucked in the woods just a couple of miles from their headquarters! It wasn't as if he was away from the rest of civilisation either, because the night before Ronnie flew back to the UK, there was a huge engagement party thrown at the American's house, and all the time one of the most wanted men in the world was hiding in one of the upstairs bedrooms, enjoying the music below and watching from his window as the hundreds of guests came and went. When morning came a van turned up to transport everybody to the airport. The van was to carry Dad, me, Veronica and Ingrid – my wife and daughter, the nanny, Chris Pickard, who is my father's biographer, Bruce Reynolds, the brain behind the train robbery, and his son Nick, and the *Sun's* seven-strong team of reporters, photographers, researchers and fixers. Bruce and Nick were there because the *Sun* wanted to buy their silence, as they knew Nick was in on it from the start and they didn't want him talking to a rival newspaper. We were all milling around as the aftermath of the party was being cleared up when we were suddenly told we couldn't use one of the main highways in Brazil, the red line, because there was a drug war going on and bullets were flying left, right and centre. The press were already waiting for us on the red line, so we used the yellow line instead. But before we got to the airport, one of the *Sun* reporters tried to prevent Veronica and Ingrid coming all the way to the airport to see us off, saying they would have to say their goodbyes there and then get out of the van. That was the last straw as far as Veronica was concerned, and she went mad. She used every bad word she knows in English, screaming at the journalist, 'You fat bastard! You dirty cunt, you cannot do that to me!' All hell was let loose in the back of the van, until suddenly I shouted, 'Everybody shut up!' Everyone was silent and I told the *Sun* journalists that if they wanted to mess with me I could still call the whole thing off.

We arrived at the main airport in Rio and the press were waiting for us at the new terminal, so we went to the old terminal and bundled out of the van. As we came into the terminal I saw two of my father's great friends, Johnny Pickston and Gio, buying their tickets to fly to London, because my Dad had suggested I had a couple of people in London who could look after me. We hurried through the terminal and as I came to the barrier I found I had about ten seconds to say goodbye to my wife and daughter. Ingrid was asleep, so I just kissed her. Veronica was in a bit of a state because she didn't know when she would see me again, and she didn't know if she would ever see Ron again. She has a lot of love for Ron and she was kissing him and saying, 'Don't worry, we'll all work it out.' To me, she said, 'Please don't leave me, take me with you.' But I didn't want her going through what I suspected was waiting for me in England; I had to protect her and Ingrid. We were taken through the barriers and into a room where we found ourselves surrounded by a load of federal police, and the British Consul in Brazil. I overheard a policeman saying, 'That's the son of the thief,' and, because I was under such stress, I had a blazing row with him, during which he threatened to arrest me. I didn't care because I wasn't prepared to take any crap from this man. In the end, the head of the federal police intervened and eventually calmed the situation down. He then took a statement from my dad which said he knew what he was doing and was leaving Brazil of his own free will. He was nice to my Dad and said, 'Mr Biggs, that neighbourhood will never be the same without you, please do come back.' I didn't like the attitude of the British Consul; he was handing out his business cards. When I asked for one, he told me he'd run out. I gave him a filthy look and wondered how the press might react if they knew he was refusing to give me one, but he must have read my mind because he suddenly found a spare card for me. My dad hit me on the arm, signalling for me to stop causing trouble. He then bent his arm and raised his fist as if to say to me, 'Fuck them.' I leaned down and whispered to him, so that the journalists and police surrounding us couldn't hear, 'Dad, pull out of this, we can walk away; you can say no, you can say no.' He wrote, 'Michael, I told you before and I am not going to tell you again, it is too late now and we are going through with this.' Had my dad wavered in any way, I would have gladly screwed the *Sun*.

I was of course really worried about my dad's well-being. I know we came in for heavy criticism for the way my father was brought back into Britain, but I have to say that had we not gone to those lengths, and he had instead been taken through the airport like a normal passenger, the whole experience would possibly have killed him because of his fragile state of health.

We finally got into the plane. It was a £40 million French-made Dassault Falcon 500 jet and it took off at precisely 9.18 p.m. British time on Sunday 6 May, 2001. Even at that point there was almost a last-minute hitch, because the wind changed direction which meant the plane could not take off at first. Kevin Crace, who brokered the deal with the Sun, told me later how he was in the *Sun*'s offices in Wapping with the editor and the staff watching the whole drama unfold on a big television screen, and they were all hanging their heads with worry because they thought we couldn't leave. But suddenly the plane was given the green light and everyone in Wapping cheered. Once we were airborne I was shocked to discover that the *Sun* – who had put him in one of their red T-shirts for the benefit of the media and camera crews – hadn't even arranged food for my dad on the plane. I had insisted they arrange for a doctor to travel with us, to help with any problems and to dispense all Dad's medication. We took off, and I looked over with concern at my dad. Here was a man who had spent the past 35 years of his life in this country, and he wasn't even looking out of the window. But I knew why he didn't want to look out of the window – he'd burst into tears, it would hurt him so much. Instead he was looking all around the plane, trying to keep himself amused, but knowing that his 13,068 days on the run were almost at an end. I was looking out at Rio, and it was a beautiful sunset. I was filming the sunset with my own video camera and thinking, will my dad ever be allowed to come back here? and when will I see my city, my wife and daughter, again? There were no certainties about what was going to happen in my life in the next few days, let alone months. The plane flew out over the Atlantic to the tiny islands of Cape Verde, hundreds of miles off the coast of Africa, where we had to land to refuel. We all disembarked to walk around in the fresh air, leaving my dad alone with Nick Reynolds on the tarmac. In the corner of the airfield there was a jeep, and Nick said to my dad, 'Ron, let's get into that jeep and fuck off. We'll go and sell the story to another paper.' My old man was amused but didn't take it seriously. We got back onto the plane and continued the long journey north, flying past Spain and France. As we approached British shores, my dad had an anxiety attack. It was only mild, and he said he just had butterflies in his stomach and felt like he might be sick, so the doctor gave him some medication.

When we touched down on Monday 7 May at RAF Airbase Northolt in north-west London, at 9 a.m., my dad and I were freaked to look out the window and see 110 policemen standing there. We were thinking, look at the amount of police they have got here, with their dogs. Afterwards I heard that Scotland Yard had planned to storm the plane if my father didn't want to get out, and they were ready to arrest me if I caused any trouble. What a stupid idea that was, and I wonder if they knew just how ridiculous they all looked. Waiting alongside them at the airfield were Dad's solicitor, Jane Wearing of Leftley Mallett Solicitors, Guy Kearl of St Paul's House Barristers' Chambers, Leeds, and Kevin Crace. Kevin said to the police chief, 'What are you guys thinking? Ronnie Biggs has come back voluntarily. In any case he is in a French plane, and you can't storm a French plane unless you have permission from their government. He's come back of his own free will, and he'll come out voluntarily. Michael won't give you any trouble, he probably just wants to walk his dad to the van and that's it, so leave them in peace.' The police then allowed Guy Kearl and Jane Wearing to board the plane, and they spent five minutes with us explaining the procedures that were to follow. Then more men entered the plane, and the police came on board to arrest my dad. Detective Chief Superintendent John Coles, head of the Flying Squad, came on board to charge him formally and read him his rights. My dad put his hand out in such a nice gesture to shake the officer's hand, and to say, 'I am Ronnie Biggs, pleased to meet you,' but the officer did not shake him by the hand. The officer just said, 'Are you Ronald Arthur Biggs? Were you born on 8 August 1929? I have here in my possession a warrant for your arrest for being unlawfully at large from HMP Wandsworth.' My dad extended his hand again, and you could hear him through his twisted mouth say the words, 'Pleased to meet you.' This time the officer had no option but to shake my father's hand. Anyone could see my father was trying to be nice, but the police officer just treated him arrogantly. Coles told my father to listen carefully as he opened a blue folder and read out the arrest warrant, reissued in 1990. It was quite a process. He said, 'I have here in my possession a warrant granted at Bow Street Magistrates' Court on 27 July 1990 for your arrest for being unlawfully at large from Her Majesty's Prison Wandsworth. Ronald Arthur Biggs, I am now going to formally arrest you on the authority of that warrant. But before I caution you or you make any form of reply I will read to you the details outlined on the warrant so that you are fully aware of the grounds upon which the arrest is made. This warrant, issued at Bow Street Magistrates' Court addressed to each and all the constables in the Metropolitan Police, accuses Ronald Arthur Biggs, address no fixed abode, of being a prisoner of Her Majesty's Prison Wandsworth, serving sentences of twenty-five and thirty years' imprisonment concurrent passed upon him at the assizes of the county of Buckingham on 16 April 1964 upon conviction of (a) conspiracy to stop mail with intent to rob the said mail and (b) robbery with aggravation, and having escaped from the said prison on the 8 July 1965, is unlawfully at large from the said prison in which he is required to be detained after being convicted of the said offences pursuant to section 72 of the Criminal Justice Act 1967. That is based on the information having been made that date from the undersigned by Detective Sgt Wilson and the accused committing the offence of the particulars above. You the said constables are hereby required to arrest the accused and bring the accused before the above magistrates' court.' Finally Coles cautioned him and said, 'You do not have to say anything but it may harm your defence if you do not mention when questioned something which you later rely on in court. Anything you do say may be given in evidence. Do you understand that?' My father nodded and at this point his barrister, Guy Kearl, advised him not to say anything. Coles finished off the arrest and asked, 'Do you wish to say anything?' My father said, 'No.' Coles said, 'Or offer any other form of reply?' Again my father said, 'No.' The policeman told us that immigration and customs officers would be coming on board to facilitate his entry into the UK. The detective added, 'You will then be taken from the plane to a waiting police vehicle and then to a London police station in anticipation of your appearance in custody before a magistrates' court. At the police station you will be examined by a doctor and will be allowed full access to your legal team. Do you understand?' My father nodded. Coles added, 'Is there anything you wish to ask me?' But my father again shook his head.

They gave me five minutes to say my goodbyes. My Dad turned to me and wrote on his pad, 'Take it easy, it will all be OK.' Then he kissed me. The police brought a camera crew in, so that Scotland Yard could show off, and then I had to walk my dad down the staircase of the plane and hand him into that van. The last thing I said to those officers was, 'Please, take it easy on him; go easy on him, he is a frail old man.' They put my dad into the van, and I saw it driving away with my father inside, heading for Chiswick Police Station in London prior to appearing at West London Court at Talgarth Road. Even then there was a scene right out of a Keystone Cops movie, as two of the rapid response vehicles leading the convoy crashed into each other as they left the airfield. I was taken back into the plane, and I started thinking, 'Maybe I shouldn't have let him come back, I have put him into jail.' I was hit with a really bad guilty feeling. What had I done?

1. SPIRIT OF THE WIND

A witch doctor once told Ronnie Biggs that, throughout his life, he was being guided by the spirit of *Inhassa*, the spirit of the winds. My father had been taken to see this spiritual priest – who belonged to the African religion of *Camdomble* – in Brazil not long after I was born, by my mother Raimunda, while the pair of them were still together. She is the daughter of an Indian, and has always been a great believer in spirits of the forest. When this spiritual father carried out the custom of throwing his shells for my father, he informed him that his saint, or the entity who looked after him, was *Inhassa*, the equivalent of Saint Barbara in Catholicism. He told my father this saint was the saint of the winds, who comes and goes, and that my father should never worry because every time he felt lonely or was in trouble, *Inhassa* would come with her wind of change and rescue him at the last minute. It was an amazing revelation, and it was true of my father's life that he always seemed to get himself out of trouble at the last possible moment. He was given all this information not long after my birth had saved him from being deported from Brazil, and he was later to have another reprieve after being kidnapped and taken to Barbados, so he could not help but believe in what the spirits had told him. It really did sum up his life; he was always the underdog in the fifteen-round fight, but always knocked out his opponent with just a matter of seconds left on the clock.

My father's first brush with the law came at the age of fifteen when he was accused of stealing pencils from Littlewoods. That was to set the pattern for Ronald Arthur Biggs. He was born on 8 August 1929, the youngest of a family of five and one of four boys. One brother, Terence, died young. During the Second World War my dad was evacuated to Devon and Cornwall, returning to London in 1942. A year later, his mother died at the age of 53 and Dad always told me that her passing had a profound effect on him. We often wondered together how his life would have turned out if she had not died at that relatively young age but had instead been around to influence his formative years.

In the same year that he first appeared in court there were two other appearances in the dock for minor theft. Maybe he decided he needed some discipline in his life because in 1947 he volunteered for the RAF. However, two years later he had a date in front of the London Sessions after the burglary of a chemist. It brought a six-month jail term and the end of his Air Force career, which had already been placed in jeopardy earlier when he went AWOL.

Dad went to Lewes Prison for Young Prisoners but one month after his release in June 1949 he was presenting himself before the North London Magistrates Court for taking a car. That booked him in for a spell in Wormwood Scrubs and then back to Lewes, which is where he first came across Bruce Reynolds. That chance meeting would have major repercussions for the rest of Dad's life, as he was set on course for a lifestyle that brought first crime and punishment, and then escape and the pursuit of his freedom. My father and Bruce shared an interest in many things, and in Lewes Prison became close friends. Bruce was particularly interested in a conversation that Dad had enjoyed with a former Post Office worker he met in Lewes who had informed him of the large sums of money transported by British Rail. He was serving eighteen months for his part in a robbery of the Post Office where he worked.

When my father had completed a four-year stretch for burglary he went and lived in Surrey with a woman who happened to be a good friend of Bruce. He had made up his mind to abandon his life of crime, get himself back on the rails and start making an honest living as a carpenter. He was bound to be impressed, however, whenever Bruce called round driving the latest sports car and always attired in smart clothes, as Bruce fancied himself a bit of a 'Raffles' of his generation. In fact, he was a walking advertisement for the slogan that crime does pay – as long as you could stay ahead of the law.

In 1958 the old man changed jobs and started work erecting partitions in offices in central London. He became familiar with the life of a commuter and on one of his train journeys he first met Charmian Powell, the daughter of a school headmaster and his wife-to-be. Things moved pretty rapidly between them and soon they were planning to elope. Charmian, after some persuading from Dad, raided the cash till at her work to provide the £200 needed to finance their adventure. With Dad's good friend Michael Haynes on board, the plan was to get to Devon and Cornwall but the funds did not extend beyond Devon. That led to a break in and arrests for all three of them, followed by Charmian's first experience of prison. She and Mike got two years' probation while Dad had to serve two-and-a-half years. It did not cool the lovers' ardour, however, and during her visits to Norwich Prison they made plans to get married. When, in December 1959, he was released from Wandsworth where he had been transferred, she was waiting outside.

Dad went back to Redhill where he had arranged to stay with friends and found work as a carpenter with Reigate Borough Council. It produced enough money to rent a small flat. Charmian spent as much time there as possible although opposition to the forthcoming union came from her father. The fact that Charmian then became pregnant was a trump card in their favour and in February 1960 they were married in Reigate register office.

The arrival of Nicholas Grant, their first son, five months later was another reason for Dad to strive to put more money into the family pot. He began working for a building contractor in Redhill which provided overtime. Later he set up his own business and within a year he had gone into partnership with Ray Stripp, who was the husband of an old school friend of Charmian. The alliance prospered to the extent that they were soon taking on help. The arrival of son number two, Christopher Dean, put more pressure on the Biggs' finances and was to lead to Dad's involvement in the raid that was to become known the world over as The Great Train Robbery, an operation revered by the criminal fraternity both for its scale and daring.

Although the business was doing well, Dad had problems with some clients who liked to drag their heels before paying their bills and he needed some help to see him over a cash crisis. He went to Bruce and asked for a loan of £500. They were old pals but on this occasion Bruce was reluctant to help. All his money was tied up in a project that he wanted Dad to be part of. They arranged to meet up and talk it over, but my father really had no plans at the time to re-enter a life of crime; he was happy going straight, playing the role of family man and building up his own business.

The robbery was to involve two established London criminal teams coming together and working as one to deprive the Post Office of the bounty contained on the Glasgow to Euston mail train. It was a wide-scale operation involving spotters in Carlisle and the gang's task was to intercept the train in Buckinghamshire. The first team had carried out a number of violent offences including robberies at a West End bank, a robbery of railway wages and another raid at the BOAC headquarters at Heathrow Airport. That was to provide the blueprint for the train robbery and was planned by Bruce and involved, among others, Charles Wilson, Roy James and Gordon Goody, who were all later involved in the train robbery.

The second team had carried out thefts of high-value cargo from trains running between London and Brighton and included Roger Cordrey as the planner. In early 1963, Brian Field, a solicitor who had prepared Goody's defence at the Airport raid, introduced Buster Edwards, the leader and organiser of the first gang, to an Ulsterman who provided information about the train that was eventually robbed. The Ulsterman has never been named. Initially Edwards intended to carry out the train robbery with his own team but he needed Cordrey's expertise because he had experience of stopping trains and robbing them. They didn't know how much was to be on the train but they were assured it was to be a larger amount than normal. How true that proved to be, as the eventual haul was the modern-day equivalent of £30 million. The High Value Package (HVP) coach would be manned by guards and there would be sorters in the other carriages. For that reason it was decided that someone had to learn to uncouple the rear carriages from the main carriage and allow the train to be driven away from the seventy or so occupants of the sorting carriage.

When Dad learned of the details from Reynolds he was not initially keen. I remember him telling me, 'I was enjoying life with a growing family and I didn't want to do anything to screw that up.' However, when he was told that there would be at least £40,000 in it for him, Dad's reluctance melted away. Forty grand was a great deal of money in 1963; enough to buy a house, enhance his business with a van and a variety of equipment, possibly pay for private education for his children while giving him and Charmian the chance to enjoy some of the high life. For that money he was also required to supply a train driver who would also be paid £40,000. By coincidence, at that time Dad was carrying out some joinery work at the Redhill home of a retired train driver. When he told Bruce that he had found a driver he also said that he wanted an equal share of the proceeds of the robbery. This didn't go down well with the sixteen members of the two gangs and there was some opposition to Dad taking part. Bruce spoke on his behalf and after a vote he was in, thrust onto a path that would change his life and his family's lives for ever. What's more, I don't suppose there would have been a Michael Biggs if he hadn't decided to join forces with Bruce and the rest of the gang.

Much of the planning had already been done. A suitable place, Bridego Bridge, was found in Buckinghamshire to bring the train to a halt. One of the gang was shown how to black out the green signal and wire up amber to force the train to slow down. Three of the gang were taught how to uncouple carriages. A nearby safe house, Leatherslade Farm, which was close to the villages of Brill and Oakley, was located and the solicitor, Brian Field, arranged the purchase. The equipment they would need included army uniforms, paint overalls and VHF radios to listen in to police messages. The range of vehicles to be used included Land Rovers, a lorry and a horsebox which would be needed to transport money from the farm.

Peter, the former train driver, was just as enthusiastic. In fact he was overwhelmed by the prospect of raking in £40,000 in exchange for driving a train a short distance. My dad went to meet the entire gang in Roy James's flat in Chelsea and learn more about the raid. He was quizzed closely about Peter, who had no experience of the criminal world. They were concerned about how he would react if arrested but Dad managed to persuade them that he would hold up. It was important for them to have somebody on board with the necessary expertise if the driver of the mail train refused to co-operate. It was crucial to have a back-up driver and, like Dad, Peter was voted in.

It needs to be stressed that there was never any intention to employ violence during the operation. If those on the train co-operated then no one needed to get hurt. A lot has been made of the injuries suffered by the train driver, Jack Mills, and the fact that he died seven years after the robbery. He put up a struggle and was hit, once, with a cosh, striking his head on the cab as he fell. My old man has always maintained that newspaper reports describing 'frenzied attacks' with an iron bar were widely off the mark and probably helped contribute to the excessive jail sentences that followed. Violence was never part of the operation and would not have occurred had Mills not decided to hurl himself at the gang member who was first into the cab. *The Times* later published a letter from Peta Fordham, the wife of the barrister who defended my father and Gordon Goody, which said Mills admitted to her that his worst injury was sustained not from the coshing, but from hitting his head against the wall of his cab as he fell. Incidentally, the man who hit Mills with the cosh was never caught or identified, along with three others including Peter, the retired driver. After Mills's death in February 1970, seven years after the robbery, the coroner stated that the cause was unrelated to injuries received in the robbery. Mills in fact died from chronic lymphatic leukaemia complicated by bronchial pneumonia.

The plan involved returning to Leatherslade Farm after the robbery and lying low until the heat had died down. They would then leave with their share of the proceeds. Some had 'tame' banks willing to accept money in false names; Dad had no specific plans in that regard but he knew a few people he could trust to look after his money if needed. The house was to be thoroughly cleaned and, if necessary, burned. In the event that didn't take place because of the police presence in the area, although some cleaning did occur. If the police happened to arrive at the farm they would be sorted out and coshes were left by the door for just that purpose.

As a cover for his absence that could last for up to two weeks, Dad concocted a story that he had to go to Wiltshire to carry out a tree-felling job. That was what he told Charmian and his work partner. Peter was going to go along as a cook and received a two-week leave of absence from his work. Instead, on the morning of Tuesday 6 August 1963, Dad took a train to Victoria Station with Peter. They met up with Bruce and other members of the gang and proceeded to

Buckinghamshire in a green army Land Rover. If they were stopped en route to the robbery their story would be that they were army personnel on night manoeuvres.

Something happened the previous day which always makes Dad chuckle. It was a bank holiday and he took Charmian and the kids on a day trip to Brighton. Before they departed, Ray arrived with money that covered some work they had carried out on a nearby house. My dad had been following the form in that morning's newspaper and decided to use that cash for a £10 wager on a couple of horses, a £5 each-way double. Dad clearly had lots on his mind and it occurred to him that it could be their last day together for a long while. Then again, all things being well, he would be returning home in two weeks' time with £40,000 in his pocket. At Brighton, Dad decided to back another horse which came in and it was while he was in the queue for his winnings that he happened to notice that day's other winners. His double hunch had come in at odds of 10-1 and 9-1, scooping Dad a not inconsiderable £500 – exactly the sum he had needed to borrow from Bruce.

On the journey to Victoria the next day Dad could not help but dwell on the irony of the situation. He had wanted to get his hands on £500 and that was the reason he was about to get involved in the raid on the mail train. Now he had got his £500 – and legally – but he was committed to the job. He also had cause to remember the words of the elderly fortune teller he had visited while on holiday in Hastings the previous year. Highly sceptical, Dad had invested in her services with some reluctance, but he was singing a different song after the visit. The woman had told him, among other things, all of which were correct, that he was a self-employed carpenter with a wife nine to ten years younger than himself and an only son who was just one year old. She said he would travel extensively around the world and would have a child with a woman with black hair. Just as Dad was leaving, she called him back and said that if ever he wanted anything in life to make sure he paid for it.

Dad, Peter and Bruce were the first to arrive at Leatherslade Farm and an Austin army truck later brought the second group including Buster Edwards. Another Land Rover brought Charlie Wilson and Roy James to the hideout. There were cards and games to while away the time and Dad was one of the first to get involved in a game of

Monopoly. The gang number rose to fifteen in the evening with the arrival of Roger Cordrey. Only Gordon Goody was absent. He was with Brian Field, waiting for the phone call from the Ulsterman, the Post Office worker in Carlisle, and the information that the extra load of cash had been put on the train. As it happened the gang had arrived a day too early – Goody got to the farm around 11 p.m. with the news that nothing was going to happen that night. That was a blow because the men were ready to spring into action. They didn't want any more hanging around than was necessary. The following day was spent idly passing time and going over the tiniest details of the operation. One moment of alarm came with a knock at the door. It was a neighbouring farmer who used to hire a meadow that was part of Leatherslade Farm and wanted to make a similar arrangement with the new 'owners'. Bruce answered the door and told him he was there to carry out some redecorating, and the neighbour accepted this.

Assuming the Ulsterman gave them the go-ahead, the gang would leave the farm just after midnight. Bruce was to be dressed like an army officer with 'official papers' in case the police happened to stop them. The rest would be kitted out like ordinary soldiers. As darkness fell, tension inside the farm rose and just before 10 p.m. Goody contacted the solicitor and returned with the news that the night mail train from Glasgow had an unusually large load on board. I remember, many years later, Dad's face would still convey his feelings of excitement and apprehension when he relayed to me the simple message that Goody passed on to the gang that fateful night in the farmhouse: 'Gentlemen, it's on its way . . .'

It was in the early hours that the convoy of two Land Rovers and the truck left Leatherslade Farm for the drive to Bridego Bridge where they were to intercept the diesel engine and twelve coaches. It was a journey of about an hour and when the gang arrived their first task was to replace the army uniforms with blue overalls, similar to those worn by rail workers. Most of them then made their way up the rail track towards Sears Crossing which, if everything went according to plan, was where the night train would be brought to a halt by a red light. After the necessary preparatory work which included the cutting of public and trackside phone lines, the gang settled down to wait for the crucial moment.

Soon after three o'clock, the voice of Bruce Reynolds came over the walkie-talkie to inform them that the train was on its way. When the red light brought it to a halt things moved rapidly. The fireman left the driver's cab to investigate and was immediately seized by two gang members and bundled down the bank in handcuffs. The train driver, Mills, put up a struggle and was hit. That was the signal for Peter to get involved and Dad led him over to the ladder which gave him access to the cab. Mills was back on his feet and Charlie Wilson was trying to console him. As things turned out Peter did not play any direct part in the robbery and nor for that matter did my father. So much for his being the master criminal! Peter's role was to drive the train and the HVP coach containing all the money – which by now had been separated from the rest of the carriages – a little further down the track. However, while he waited for the brake pressure to build some of the gang began to panic and elbowed Peter out of the way, installing Mills behind the wheel once more with the threat of the cosh if he didn't obey orders. After that mini crisis the train was on its way, drawing up, as arranged, at Bridego Bridge where Reynolds was waiting. Dad took Peter back to the Land Rover where they sat and watched the rest of the gang remove the mailbags and put them into the truck. Dad did not assist in the break-in to the carriage and neither was he involved in the unloading and the loading at the scene. Peter was not happy. He had wanted to do his bit for the gang and was annoyed that he had not been allowed to drive away the train. Incredibly, the whole operation from the moment when the train was brought to a halt to when the last bag was loaded onto the truck lasted less than forty minutes, and before long the convoy was heading back to the farm. Dawn was breaking as they made their final approach and as it happened that day was also Dad's birthday. At that moment life could not have held any better prospects for a 35-year-old carpenter.

The truck was parked out of the way in a lean-to shed and the Land Rovers were placed out of sight. It would have been impossible to tell that the farmhouse was occupied. Inside began the enjoyable task of counting the money as 120 mailbags were dumped on to the living-room floor and opened. It took Dad, Bruce and one other gang member nearly three hours to empty the sacks before the count could begin. Charlie Wilson and Roger Cordrey were appointed 'accountants' to take responsibility for the counting and distribution of the cash. Others were on lookout duty or monitoring the police traffic on the radio. When the magical million pound mark was reached there was much whooping of delight. Those not on lookout duty resumed the game of Monopoly, probably thinking about using the real money for their little game, now that they had enough of it.

Around midday the gang were given food for thought when the radio carried information that police believed army vehicles had been used in the raid and that the culprits were probably hiding in a nearby farmhouse. That changed the plans considerably because originally the idea was to stay at Leatherslade Farm for as long as a week. The count was almost complete and the pile had swollen to a value of more than £2,500,000. According to the Guinness Book of Records the total haul that night was £2,631,784 of which only £343,448 was ever recovered. After Peter was given his £40,000 the money was split equally between the rest of the gang members and Dad put his share into two army kitbags, holdalls and suitcases. It amounted to more than £147,000 – not bad for a night's work. Now came the question of how to get away. The general consensus was that they needed to move and move quickly, although nothing could be done until the next day. The rest of that day was spent drinking warm beer. As it was Dad's birthday, each of the gang made a point of handing him over a five-pound note as a present.

The following day saw a flurry of activity as the urgency to evacuate mounted. The news broadcasts indicated that the police were certain the perpetrators were still in the area and a massive search was being organised which would cover a thirty-mile radius from the robbery site. Leatherslade Farm fell just inside that area. Cars arrived to spirit the gang away and Dad travelled with Bruce to Redhill, relieved to get a safe passage through the country lanes without any sign of the police. At Heathrow he telephoned Charmian to say he was on his way back. It was clear from the question she posed him that she had a fair idea what he'd been up to. His first move on arriving back home was to deposit the two kitbags on the kitchen floor and pull out a bundle of notes for Charmian. Bruce left and he and Dad did not see each other again for 29 years. Charmian had some news of her own. Dad's elder brother Jack had died of a heart attack on the eve of the robbery. They had tried to locate Dad in Wiltshire but, obviously, to no avail.

Dad arranged for three 'minders' to babysit the money. A small amount went on a belated birthday celebration in London while Charmian enjoyed a shopping spree with the £500 Dad had won on the horses. For the moment life was good and there was much to enjoy and look forward to but the net was beginning to tighten. A farm labourer had tipped off the police about a suspicious-looking truck parked in a farm less than thirty miles from the robbery and on 13 August the police called there. The following evening Dad heard that Roger Cordrey had been arrested. He had tried to rent a flat from a policeman's widow and had paid three months' rent in advance in cash which made her suspicious. A week later Charlie Wilson was arrested and Scotland Yard circulated pictures of several others including Bruce and Buster Edwards. As someone who had associated with Bruce in Wandsworth Prison, Dad knew that he could expect a visit from the police sooner rather than later. Sure enough, on 24 August, came a knock on the door and a visit from two officers from Reigate Station. They asked Dad about Bruce Reynolds and when they had last seen each other. My father said it had been four years, when they were in Wandsworth together. The police checked out every room and even had a look into the coal shed. They went on their way, apparently satisfied that Dad was not involved, although they did ask him to tip them off if Reynolds should come calling.

As August came to an end the robbery was dominating the papers less and less. Dad began to relax a bit more but then in early September he arrived home to find two police officers in his kitchen. They were flourishing a search warrant and indicating that they were about to take up the floorboards. A cupboard where Dad used to keep tins of paint also aroused the officers' interest a great deal. Eventually Dad was hauled off to Scotland Yard where, after a couple of initial questions, he was charged with the robbery. Suddenly all those lovely blue five-pound notes and the lifestyle they could fund seemed an awfully long way away. The next, unwanted, phase of Dad's life was about to begin.

Dad was remanded in Bedford Prison along with Charlie Wilson and Roger Cordrey. Others came and joined them at different intervals. Buster Edwards and Bruce Reynolds were both being sought but had escaped capture so far (it wasn't until September 1966 that Edwards was arrested after turning himself in, while Reynolds wasn't arrested until November 1968 in Torquay). In Bedford Prison much discussion took place between the men of what evidence was being compiled against them. Fingerprinting was debated and thrown out but there was cause soon enough to recall that Monopoly game with some distaste, as the set had not been properly disposed of and the ones who had not worn gloves had left their dabs all over it. Dad tried to drum up interest in an escape but such was the confidence among the others that they would get off that only Charlie Wilson and Gordon Goody were ready to make a break with him. They were transferred to Aylesbury Prison and began the long wait for their cases to come to trial. One possible escape attempt that involved administering drugs to the prison officers was halted when the severity of the penalties for such an offence was considered. Another plot foundered when Bill Boal got cold feet at the last minute and put to waste all the effort that had already gone into producing dummy keys and organising a getaway car.

The trial began on 20 January 1964, the council chamber in Aylesbury being converted into a courtroom to accommodate all the accused. The court heard that Dad's fingerprints had been found on a Pyrex bowl, a bottle of ketchup and the Monopoly set discovered at Leatherslade Farm. The evidence of the train driver, Jack Mills, made a big impression on the court. He later revealed in a book that he was told not to admit under any circumstances that his most serious head injury had come from his fall and not from the blow from the cosh. When Detective Inspector Basil Morris of Reigate CID appeared at court to give evidence he let on that Dad had said under questioning that he had met Bruce Reynolds in jail. This was an error because no indication should be given to the jury that any of the accused had done time as their verdict could be influenced. My father demanded a retrial and got it. It was a boost for him because he believed he stood a better chance if he stood accused on his own rather than with the others. He was discharged and returned to custody to await a new trial.

Meanwhile, back in the courtroom, all manner of excuses were being produced for why fingerprints were found in the farmhouse. Nevertheless, all the accused – with the exception of John Wheater, the solicitor Brian Field worked for – were found guilty of conspiring to stop a mail train with intent to rob and several were also found guilty of robbery with violence. Sentence was deferred until after Dad's retrial. His case was that he had been offered the chance to buy the house they were renting in Redhill. He needed £500 as a deposit and became aware, through an old prison pal, of a job out in the country. The cover was that he was going to Wiltshire to take part in some tree-felling exercise which would produce the money he needed. Instead of driving to Wiltshire they were taken to Leatherslade Farm where the presence of army uniforms had alerted Dad to the existence of a possible plan to attack a military installation. He wanted no part of that but while at the farm he organised himself a meal and later passed time with a game of Monopoly. That explained the existence of his fingerprints. After that they headed to London where Dad stayed with a friend before returning to Redhill.

The story did not convince the Jury and Dad was found guilty on both counts. The sentences were outrageously lengthy, Mr Justice Davies laying down terms of 25 years for the conspiracy charge and thirty for the robbery with violence, the sentences to run concurrently. It was a huge stretch and, as Dad was taken down, he had cause to reflect that even with good behaviour his next twenty years would be spent behind bars – twice the amount he would have got had he actually killed someone. The only consolation as he headed off to Her Majesty's Prison in Lincoln was the possibility of a parole system being introduced which could knock one third off the sentence. It was a straw to clutch at; the sentence, he told himself, had obviously been set so high with that in mind. Maybe in ten years or so he would be a free man. Little did he know then of the adventures that lay ahead.

2. SYDNEY TO SUGAR LOAF

Appeals were lodged against the severity of the jail sentences. Some were lucky and their terms of imprisonment were reduced, but not my father. The very same day he was transferred to Wandsworth Prison, a place he knew well and which he could not recall with any fondness. A clear-headed analysis of his future would have concluded that it was to be his home for the next twenty years but, as things turned out, he was only there for a few days over a year.

The old man's initial intention was to serve his ten years and then take advantage of the parole system which he was convinced was going to be introduced. So to begin with he wasn't interested in any suggestions of escape and told a fellow inmate by the name of Paul Seabourne, who was offering to help 'spring' him, that he would do his ten years and take advantage of parole. This other prisoner told him he was living in dreamland – there had been talk of a parole scheme for years and nothing had come of it. Reality slowly began to dawn and as a result he became more and more receptive to any suggestions of escape.

The two became firm friends and it emerged that Paul – who was soon to be released – was motivated by a sense of injustice about my dad's length of sentence. He was like a dog with a bone and wouldn't let go until he had accomplished what he believed was my father's only rightful response to the authorities – escape.

There was one drawback. Charlie Wilson got away from HMP Winson Green and that resulted in an increase in security as far as the Great Train Robbery gang were concerned. Prison officers escorted my dad everywhere he went and it led to him making a request to the governor to relax the attention because it was getting him down. When it was refused he immediately went out to the exercise yard and informed Paul that he was ready to break out.

Various ruses were planned and discussed. An old friend, a helicopter pilot, arrived at Wandsworth and offered his services in an airborne lift, but as far as my father was concerned that carried too much risk. He was far more keen on an alternative scheme which involved the use of a removal van. Another friend had arrived at the jail and he was included in the escape plan. The idea was to strike during one of the two hour-long exercise periods in the afternoon. The help of one or two friendly cons was enlisted to deal with those prison officers who would be out in the yard when zero hour arrived.

When Paul got his release from jail he went to work in earnest on completing preparations. The day originally set aside for the escape turned out to be wet and so the plan was shelved for 24 hours. The following morning, 8 July 1965, one year and eleven months since the day of the robbery, dawned bright and sunny and Charmian went off to Whipsnade Zoo with the children, all excited at the prospect of seeing their father again. In the exercise yard at the allotted time Dad heard the sound of a large vehicle drawing up on the other side. He stopped to tie up his laces, looking up at the wall at the same time, and at that moment a head in a nylon stocking appeared, closely followed by a rope ladder cascading down the wall. Along with another con who was in on the escape, an old acquaintance named Eric Flower, my father made a beeline for the ladder while the 'minders' took care of the officers.

Once over the wall the two escapees dropped down into the van which had been parked close to the wall. Old mattresses cushioned their fall. A getaway car was parked nearby and away they went, Dad and Eric, Paul and two others involved in the escape as well as two opportunist cons who had taken advantage of the situation and seized their chance to get up and over the wall. In a cul-de-sac close to the prison they transferred to a second car and from there motored on to Dulwich, where the other two inmates scarpered and Dad, Eric and Paul went to their hideout – the upstairs flat of a semi-detached house in a quiet side-street. Out came the champagne. Freedom tasted just great.

Eric's concern was that the police would quickly be all over south London and he was anxious to move on. When it was dark he nipped out to make a telephone call and arranged for a couple of friends from east London to come over and ferry them to Bermondsey, where they stayed holed up in a tenement building for a few days. After a week

SYDNEY TO SUGAR LOAF

there, my father's next home became a spacious apartment in Camberwell where he was introduced to a man who could take care of travel arrangements involving temporary passports, a boat to Europe and even plastic surgery in Paris with real passports and airline tickets from there onwards. It would all take time, however, and meanwhile it was considered best to move on again, this time to an apartment between Richmond and Putney.

In all the time since the escape, Dad had not seen Charmian and the only contact he was able to make with his wife was via the telephone, but an advertisement which featured a three-bedroom place in Bognor Regis offered the prospect of a proper meeting with loved ones. Both Dad and Eric were keen and arranged the deal. Sunbathing in the garden made for a more relaxed existence and Eric's wife Carol came down to take care of the domestic chores. Then one night, Charmian arrived with the kids – Dad was made up.

After three months of lying low the time was approaching when they would try and flee the country. Eric and Dad went back to Camberwell where instructions soon arrived for their escape across the North Sea. Eric and my father were handed seamen's clothes and put in a black van en route to the coast. After an uncomfortable journey in the hold of a vessel surrounded by sacks of rubber they docked in Antwerp and were taken to a motel where the plans were laid out for them to journey on to Paris.

Crossing the border into France was no problem as Dad – now with a passport in the name of Ronald King – slept in the back of a car along with the two young daughters of an English couple who were in the front seats. Once in Paris he and Eric headed for a fourth-floor apartment where they were to be in the care of 'Henri', a big-hearted, powerful man in his mid fifties. At this stage my dad was still undecided about where their final destination should be. He could not rid himself of the memory of the old Seekers hit single which told of the delights of Australia, and his mind was made up when, on a Sunday afternoon, he came across an article extolling the delights of that country and, in particular, Bondi Beach. Luckily Eric was in full agreement that it should be the place for them to go.

First though they both had to take on new appearances, courtesy of a man who was said to be one of the best cosmetic surgeons on the continent. As far as he was concerned his two patients were a couple of tax dodgers from Canada. It was quite an ordeal, Dad describing it as pain he had never experienced before and on more than one occasion he had to resist the strong urge to throw himself out of the window and onto the street below. The results were successful eventually and before long new passports had arrived, plus a ticket to Australia for Eric who, it had been decided, would fly to Sydney two days before my dad. A Christmas present arrived for him in Paris in the shape of Charmian and the boys who were at first taken aback by their father's new look. It was a good sign that the surgeon's handiwork had been successful and that all the pain was worthwhile.

On 29 December 1965 Dad's new passport, in the name of Terence Furminger, and a ticket to Sydney arrived. Dad was turning his back on Europe and his family although the plan was for Charmian and the kids to join him as soon as possible. He touched down in Australia on New Year's Eve and the sense of freedom wrapped around him like a favourite old overcoat. Not even the rain that greeted him that first day could dampen the characteristic Ronnie Biggs spirit. Life was great and it felt wonderful not having to keep looking over his shoulder the whole time. The one slightly disconcerting thing was that Eric was not at the hotel where the two had arranged to meet, but Dad was soon putting his concern aside with a night on the town, getting stuck into the liquor and mixing with an assortment of British sailors and their girlfriends. The champagne combined well with the raucous singing and a good time was had by all.

The following night, after a day spent in the company of a friendly taxi driver which included a visit to the races and a Chinese restaurant, Dad was contacted by Eric, who had already found employment as a petrol-pump attendant and was in the habit of going each morning to the beach. It was all a far cry from the privations of Wandsworth Prison. They found themselves a house in Botany Bay and the taxi driver agreed to receive their mail. The money from the Train Robbery quickly ran out and Charmian was asked to send more through the post; this involved a careful procedure in which the money was hidden inside magazines. The second delivery caught the attention of Post

Office inspectors who made it clear that they would like to find out why money was being mailed in this fashion from England.

It was the cue for Dad and Eric to make a hasty retreat out of Sydney and they headed first to Melbourne and then on to Adelaide. Again, initial impressions were favourable and they felt immediately at home, finding rooms in a guest house. Eric resumed work as a petrol attendant while Dad reintroduced himself to his skills as a joiner, working in a furniture factory. All things considered, theirs was not a bad lot.

Information reached them that Eric's wife and daughter had arrived in Sydney and they drove to meet them. They had brought a letter from Charmian which included more funds and the news that she would be flying in herself in the next couple of months. Her arrival made for a particularly stressful time for my father. To be on the safe side it was agreed that she would go to Darwin but he was late getting to the airport to meet her and when he finally arrived he caught sight of her in an office talking with officials. Dad assumed she had been apprehended, presumably for being in possession of a false passport, and began to panic. He telephoned Eric who suggested that he beat a hasty retreat and get back to Adelaide, but Dad stayed in Darwin and discovered that a Mrs Margaret Furminger had indeed arrived and was staying at the Fanny Bay Hotel. Dad took a taxi there where his apprehension was not helped by the presence a number of plain-clothes policemen in and around the hotel. He was convinced that as soon as he asked for Mrs Furminger, that would be that, and he would be back in custody. However, nobody reacted to his query at the reception desk and very quickly Charmian and the kids were hurrying down the stairs and into his embrace. It turned out that so many police were around because Darwin was hosting a big convention for the force which had made hotel rooms scarce at that time, and Charmian's discussions with officials at the airport, which Dad had witnessed and immediately jumped to the wrong conclusion about, were because she was seeking help with somewhere to stay.

Charmian had brought with her the £7,000 which was all that remained of my father's share of the bounty. The rest had gone on paying for the escape, the new identities, and all the travel. With the money they bought a station wagon and loaded it with provisions, with the idea of making a slow journey to Adelaide. They had a whale of a time stopping over at Alice Springs and then making a detour to Cairns, going via Sydney and Melbourne before arriving in Adelaide. In all they were on the road for just over a month and in that time Charmian found herself pregnant again.

Back in Adelaide they linked up again with Eric and his family. Dad rented a big family house and resumed work as a carpenter. He did plenty of overtime and money was not a problem. The children enjoyed the lifestyle and the beach culture went down a treat with all concerned. Their third son, Farley Paul, was born on 27 April 1967, but the joy of his arrival proved to be short-lived as a letter soon arrived, anonymously, carrying the distressing news that the police somehow knew of my father's existence in Australia. It puzzled them how anyone had their address because it was known to only a few and they were all close friends, and Dad had to be persuaded that they had to move on, although his initial reaction had been to ignore it.

In the dead of night my father and Eric drove out of Adelaide with a truck laden with as many belongings as they could put on board, destination Melbourne, with the mothers and children staying behind in Adelaide. In Melbourne it did not take too much trouble to find a two-bedroom house that was available to rent and then it was back to Adelaide to pick up Charmian and the kids. In Melbourne Dad was to be known as Terry Cook and Charmian as Sharon. Eric and his wife stayed behind in Adelaide but making new friends did not prove difficult. Dad changed his job on a number of occasions, always looking for the best opportunity as far as overtime was concerned. From time to time the newscasts would include details of the train gang and their arrests; Buster Edwards turned himself in and in January 1968 they discovered that Charlie Wilson had been captured. Every time the robbery was mentioned in news bulletins like that it had a bad effect on the old man, because even though he was thousands of miles from home it made him feel less secure.

The chance discovery that old friends Mike and Jessie Haynes had emigrated to Australia and were living and working in Melbourne brightened the horizon considerably, but for every patch of blue sky there was a dark cloud around the corner and the one that arrived on 8 November 1969 carried details of Bruce Reynolds's arrest in

Torquay. That set in motion a sequence of events that were to have serious repercussions for Dad and were to put an end to his life in Oz. Bruce's wife did a newspaper article which was reprinted in an Australian women's magazine. Young Nicky saw it and pointed it out to his mum, saying, 'There's a picture of Dad.'

Naturally my father was not best pleased when he returned home and saw the article, even less so when one of the guests at the house that he and Eric had stayed in also saw it and was convinced that one of the wanted men pictured on the page was Terry King. She showed it to a friend who just happened to be a broadcaster on a small radio station near Perth and he helpfully decided to make his suspicions known on air! Naturally he received a visit from the police who also took an interest in Terry King. The development hardly pleased Eric either. He had joined forces again with his two pals from east London who had provided accommodation following the Wandsworth break-out. They had set up a trucking company in Adelaide and were doing well but on learning of the magazine article they decided they had to move out, advising Dad to do the same, and this was before they'd heard of the problem the newscaster had stirred up. However, Dad was intent on letting the storm abate and decided to stay put. Meanwhile, Eric and his pals went to Sydney.

Dad changed his job and became a foreman in a company dealing in suspended ceilings and office partitions. He was popular at work and a much-loved father at home where, with Charmian out at work, the children used to cherish their time with him in the evenings. There was so much to enjoy about their lifestyle – if only the law men would leave them be. On one October evening a telephone call came through from an Australian friend who knew my father's real identity. He advised him to watch the news bulletins which carried details of a memo which had been seen at Melbourne's police headquarters and which stated that Dad was thought to be living there with his wife and children. Pictures of Dad and Eric were shown; the net was beginning to close.

Dad was tired of running away and wanted to stay put, but Charmian insisted he had to move on again and together they agreed that he would go and stay in a hotel on the outskirts of the city and lie low until the fuss began to die down. Dad went out to lunch and picked up a newspaper which included his picture in a front page story and details of how Charmian had returned to their home to be met by a posse of armed police. The firearms unnerved Charmian and it was clear they wanted Dad – dead or alive. She was locked up in the police station and the children put into a home. The plan had been for Dad and Charmian to meet up that evening in a Chinese restaurant. Not knowing what had happened to his wife, he still intended to make the appointment although when he left the hotel he took his belongings with him, convinced he would not be returning. When Charmian did not appear he guessed what had happened. The question now was where was he going to go?

He decided to seek the help of the Australian friend who had tipped him off the previous evening. He knocked on the bedroom window and gave him the fright of his life but was welcomed in and then he made arrangements for my father to hole up in a little holiday home high up in the Melbourne mountains. He was well looked after there and was cheered up considerably by the news that Charmian had been released from prison and was back with the kids. Later Dad's friend told him that she had sold her story to the newspapers for $65,000, so at least she had some money to tide her over. However, there was no chance of Dad dropping his guard. The police were anxious to get their high-profile fugitive behind bars and airports and railway stations were being closely monitored while road blocks were also in operation. A few days later the television bulletin provided the news that the police were going to switch their hunt to the mountains, and Dad's Aussie friend was soon knocking on his door. He was running out of places to go and it was then that he turned to his old friend Mike Haynes. He had nearly gone there before but decided against it, fearing that the police had the property under close watch.

When Dad knocked on his door, Mike was relieved because he had been expecting the law. He knew a young English couple who could put Dad up for a week or two. Under cover of darkness the next night Dad was taken to his new hideaway where he was shown everything he might need. During the day he would have to fend for himself as both were out at work and through the net curtains he spied patrol cars cruising the neighbourhood. Luckily a break-out at the

Melbourne jail took the focus away from him for a while, though the news that Eric Flower had been arrested in Sydney was not welcomed. The weeks passed and still the old man continued to evade the authorities. The Haynes had not been visited by police so Dad decided it was safe to move in with them. If he could stay put for a few months then he would investigate making his way up north. With the help of friends he was able to communicate with Charmian but it was a risky business because the police had her under close watch and a patrol car could always be seen close to her home.

Christmas was a particularly miserable time for Dad as he was unable to see the people most dear to him, but he couldn't really complain. The alternative was no option at all and his circle of friends in Australia were doing everything they could for him. Mike Haynes suggested that Dad might like to use his passport, a feasible suggestion because the two men were quite similar in height and appearance. Dad would have to be disguised to get out of the country and it was agreed that he would continue to add to the weight that had been piling on since he first went on the run in Australia. From then on it was spaghetti bolognese on the menu every single day.

When Jessie returned home one day clutching a raft of travel brochures she told Dad to pick out his next destination. Top of the pile was a picture of Sugar Loaf Mountain and the Bay of Guanabara and Dad had no need to look any further. None of the party knew anything about South America other than the fact that it was a convenient hideout for Nazi war criminals and full of corrupt officials – it sounded ideal! A boat trip to Panama followed by a plane journey to Rio de Janeiro would do the trick.

Dad needed to work on Mike's passport and, luckily, his photograph was easy to remove, but the difficult part was reproducing the Foreign Office stamp which is found on the bottom right-hand corner of the picture. Dad got himself a couple of dozen passport pictures and then persuaded the Haynes family to make themselves scarce for the weekend while he applied total concentration to the task in hand. It proved to be successful work and by the end there was a genuine-looking passport for the new Michael Haynes. Mike was certainly impressed by the finished article – perhaps Dad should have taken up forgery before. Charmian had managed to get her hands on a cash advance for the story she had sold to the papers and that gave Dad a little money for the trip. When Jessie went and sorted out his ticket to Panama on a Greek liner, my father's stay in Australia had only a week to run.

Departure day, 5 February 1970, dawned with my father naturally feeling apprehensive; he had enjoyed his time in Australia and had made a lot of friends there. The willingness of people to come to his aid and offer him safe refuge when the police were closing in was particularly touching, but more than anything there was sadness at the thought of saying his goodbyes to Charmian and the boys. In Dad's situation you never knew if it would be the final goodbye. For her part Charmian was relieved at the prospect that Dad would have a little respite after months of living on the edge, never knowing if the knock at the door was the fateful one, or if a police posse lay in wait around the street corner.

Fortunately the ship was to set sail at night so Dad was able to leave the house under cover of darkness. The plan was that Mike would go through passport control as if he was the passenger while Dad and Jessie went aboard as visitors to say their final farewells. Mike's picture had been put back loosely in the passport and once they were all on board, Dad would take the ticket and passport, replace the photographs, and off he would go. Everything went as planned. Mike got through passport control without a hitch and Dad, resplendent in horn-rimmed glasses and a checked cap, walked up the gangplank with Jessie steadying herself on his arm. Dad took the passport and ticket from Mike and then went to find his cabin where he swapped the pictures, flushing Mike's torn-up photo down the toilet. He said his farewells to Mike and Jessie with a large lump in his throat. He was on his own again and off to pastures new.

3. SAMBA!

My Dad was sharing a cabin on board the SS *Ellinis* with a couple of Australian university students who were making their way to Canada, and an Italian-Yugoslav called Peter, who was also heading for Canada. With the assistance of copious amounts of drink that first evening the cabin colleagues quickly got to know one another. It was never far from Dad's mind that someone might see through the disguise but next morning, as he took a stroll on deck, he was reassured to discover that no one was paying him any special attention. True to form he found himself alongside a pretty Australian woman at breakfast. As others joined them it became hotter in the restaurant and my father began encountering problems with his glasses which kept sliding down his nose and eventually fell onto his plate. He cursed them, placed them in his pocket and vowed never to use them again.

Sydney was the first stop and the two university lads, Bill and Greg, wanted to go ashore and carry on where the party had left off. The old man, claiming he was feeling sick after the excesses of the night before, bowed out – he didn't want any alert Aussies ruining his plans at this stage. After Sydney the next stop was New Zealand and, as the ship passed beneath Sydney Harbour Bridge and a chorus of 'Waltzin' Matilda' rang out among all the passengers, the old man was so cut up he couldn't join in. He felt he would never see Australia again and he knew he was going to miss it badly.

In New Zealand 'Mike Haynes' was again reluctant to leave the ship but his cabin mates and others he had got to know insisted that he joined them. A pair of sunglasses came in handy and helped my Dad feel more at ease, although he was still very much on his guard. Back on board later that night he attended the Captain's Party where an English girl in a white dress, called Molly, caught his eye. They struck up a friendship and one morning she worried him by suddenly turning and whispering to him that she knew who he really was. Apparently she thought he was Bruce Reynolds and Dad feigned outrage and said that she would find that Reynolds was being detained at Her Majesty's pleasure for the Great Train Robbery. Molly's reply was that in that case he must be Charlie Wilson, or if not Charlie Wilson then Ronnie Biggs. 'Yes, that's who you are,' said Molly. 'But don't worry, I won't tell anyone.' It was an amazing exchange but if she really did suspect his real identity then Dad knew that he could trust her not to give the game away.

After docking at Tahiti the ship then made tracks for Panama where my father would disembark and say his goodbyes to most of his new-found friends who were going on to England, Canada and the USA. Immigration officials joined the ship to interview those who were leaving and he was told that he did not have a visa to land there. He was forced to pay a bond of a couple of hundred dollars which was to be repaid if he could show the authorities an airline ticket out of Panama. That created a problem as he needed that money to pay for his ticket to Rio de Janeiro. Just at that moment an announcement came over the loudspeaker that my Dad was wanted in the Purser's office, causing another shiver of fear to shoot through his mind. Fortunately it was only good news; Charmian had managed to wire on to the ship a further $200 so his immediate prayers were answered. By now Molly had become quite attached to Dad and was talking in terms of staying with him in Panama and abandoning her plans to return to England and be reunited with her boyfriend. Dad insisted that she get back on the boat because the life that awaited her in England was what she was really cut out for, not a life on the run in South America with a middle-aged man.

Before my Dad reached his final destination of Rio there was one more stopover. Two of his circle of friends on the *Ellinis* who had also embarked in Panama, a Spaniard called Frank and his German friend Rosie, had invited Dad to join them in Venezuela where Frank was going to live with his brother. It proved an enjoyable two-week stay and with Frank at work he spent a lot of time with Rosie who was starting a new life in South America after leaving her husband in Australia. She wanted my father to stay on and, as there was also the offer of a job, he was tempted but the plan all along had been to get to Brazil and nothing was going to stand in the way.

Arrival day in the Brazilian capital was Sunday 11 March 1970, a few weeks before Pele and his famous team of talented Brazilian footballers lifted the World Cup for Brazil, defeating England along the way. Even early in the morning it was hot and sunny and Dad told me how he remembered having the same feelings of excitement and anticipation setting foot on the soil here for the first time as he did when he first entered Australia. Passing through immigration control was a breeze and for the first time in a long, long while my father found himself relaxing. He had struck up conversation on the plane with an elderly American called Bill who was heading for Argentina but was stopping en route to deliver a letter in Rio to a friend of his wife. He had a hotel booked on the Copacabana seafront and suggested that Dad try and find a room there as well. The drive from the airport along Botafogo Beach brought into view the spectacular sights that had first attracted my father's attention on the brochure he had been given by Jessie Haynes in Melbourne.

Getting to grips with normal day-to-day life in Rio proved difficult because of the language barrier. When Bill departed Dad knew of no other English-speaking person there apart from Bill's friend Nadine Mitchell, a striking American lady and the widow of a Brazilian army colonel. Through her he met a young Australian, Rob, who shared Dad's love of strong liquor, and a friendly Swiss couple, Werner and Joyce Blumer, who offered him some carpentry work and eventually a room in their house. At the same time Dad was forming a close relationship with Edith, sister-in-law of Adauto, a young clerk he had befriended at the American Express office. He trusted Edith enough to tell her his story, including the fact that he had a wife and children in Australia.

After six months my father had to renew his visa, a requirement that meant he would have to leave the country if only for a short time. He decided to take a coach journey to Argentina which seemed like a good idea at the time but turned out instead almost to be his undoing. It got off to a bad start when he found himself sitting next to a very large Brazilian lady who began to encroach onto his seat, thus making any hope of sleep impossible. Changing buses at Porto Alegre brought more disaster as the vehicle skidded on a muddy road, ending up in a ditch whereupon all the men were required to get out and help coax the bus back onto the highway. Dad's mood was not helped when the driver mistakenly hit the accelerator pedal, sending the bus violently back towards the ditch. He leaped out of the way and landed up to his knees in red mud. Getting into Argentina proved nerve-racking as the immigration official took a particular interest in his passport, particularly the page that showed Michael Haynes had crossed into Pakistan from India and was suspected of trying to smuggle in a Land Rover; there was some kind of red stamp in a foreign language that Dad had never looked at carefully which explained this. He barked out something in Spanish which drew a blank response from my father and eventually his passport was handed back. Accommodation had been arranged through Fanny, an Argentine friend of Nadine, and he was fixed up with her relatives in Buenos Aires. With money running out, and the temperatures none too welcoming, a week's stay was plenty, and very soon he was back on the road to Rio, though on a different route to his outward journey because he didn't want to come into contact with that suspicious passport official again.

Back in Rio things were slowly coming together for Dad and extra work came in from Scott Johnson, an American colleague of Werner Blumer, who was also in need of a carpenter. Scott also proved useful as an entrance ticket to the samba clubs that proliferate in the Brazilian capital. He was quite well off and popular with the women and Dad found no hardship in sharing his company. With the hours he was working the old man was able to set his sights a little higher and could begin to afford some small luxuries. He had picked out an apartment of his own in Copacabana owned by one of Scott's friends which was available for a small rent. Dad was writing to Charmian and they were making vague plans to meet up again, possibly with Dad getting back into Australia. For that reason it was important to keep his passport up to date.

One day in February 1971 a telephone call came through from Adauto saying that a letter had arrived for Dad at the American Express office. The handwriting was Charmian's but Dad's joyful anticipation of more money or warm family greetings were cruelly cut short by the opening line of her letter which implored him to sit down before he read any further. Greatly shocked, he read that their son Nicky had been killed in a road accident. It had happened after Charmian had dropped the Haynes off at their home and her car was hit by another vehicle going across the junction. Although Charmian blamed herself, it had been her right of way. She and Chris were severely shaken and Farley badly cut but Nicky had taken the brunt of the collision. So grievous was the blow that Dad reeled in and out of a bar, having stumbled for words as he attempted to call Adauto. He had felt a burning desire to talk to someone but then could not find the means to speak once Adauto had answered. His mind was made up – he would turn himself in to the authorities at the British Consulate. A short while later he found himself standing outside the Consulate in Flamengo, but in the meantime he had begun to come to his senses and was starting to counsel himself against doing anything rash. After a couple of brandies and a period of reflection on a park bench, the old man came to the conclusion that the last thing he should do was give himself up because he knew that was not what Nicky would have wanted.

It was clear from Dad's demeanour that something terrible had happened but he invented a story to deflect the Blumers' concern. They had no idea he had a wife and three children on the other side of the world and he thought it best to keep that sort of information secret. Returning to Australia figured more and more in Dad's thoughts and, in order to keep his passport up to date, he had to take a second trip out of Brazil. Reluctant to make a return visit to Argentina, he decided to take a bus trip to the Bolivian border. After at least half-a-dozen stops while police examined the passengers' identity and travel documents, he wished he hadn't, but he accomplished what he had set out to do and the visa was revalidated.

On his return he moved into a twelfth-floor apartment a short distance from the Copacabana beach. The pain of Nicky's death took a long while to ease but gradually he got his life back together, spending time on the beach with Edith and her friends. When Edith was away on a long holiday to England and America, Dad took to visiting Adauto's jazz sessions again and was introduced to a Brazilian called Paulo who took my father to his favourite club, the Bola Preta in downtown Rio. There he noticed an exotic young dancer with long black hair whose name was Raimunda Nascimento de Castro. She had a wonderful smile and after exchanging a few words she agreed to meet my father at the club the following week. Most of Dad's women friends came in and out of his life with some rapidity but Raimunda was different and their relationship was to have a profound effect for Dad – and also for me!

They got on well but things came to a head the day before Edith was to due to return, when Dad suggested that Raimunda remove a nightdress that had been left on a bed. Raimunda didn't take kindly to that and told Dad he had to make a choice between Edith and her. The decision went in Edith's favour and Raimunda stormed off in a huff. However, something had changed in Dad's relationship with Edith and she made it clear soon after her return from New York that she would be going back there for her next vacation. She failed to return for Dad's birthday as she had promised and when he telephoned her sister to try and find where she might be he was astonished to discover that she had gone and got married in New York to a German man she had met there the previous year. By this stage my father had decided not to return to Australia and had allowed the validity of his passport to expire. It no longer seemed such a good idea to go back there because he believed it would only be disruptive to Chris and Farley who were at school and leading ordered lives. Naturally Charmian was not happy at his decision.

Dad was not one for wasting time and, while Edith was away, he and Scott went back to Bola Preta where the old man got dancing with an attractive girl called Ana Paula. Out of the blue Raimunda came back into Dad's life which almost caused another angry scene as she and Ana Paula almost came face to face as they went to visit him. The relationship with Ana Paula came to an amicable end and Raimunda moved into his apartment. At an appropriate moment he told her all about Charmian and their kids, and she accepted it without turning a hair. She herself had a young son by a doctor who was living in northern Brazil.

The old man received word from Mike Haynes that he wanted his passport back. His request to the Australian authorities for a replacement, claiming he had lost his old one, was rejected and he was told he had to find it. Luckily, Dad was introduced to a girl who worked in tourism and who was taking charge of a group of Brazilians travelling to Australia. He arranged for her to take presents for his friends in Australia and included Mike's passport in among them.

More people came into Dad's life – male as well as female – and Raimunda kept him on his toes, at one time bringing her mother and her fifteen-year-old adopted daughter to stay in the apartment. The two new residents were happy to sleep in the lounge but it did not make for happy relations and before long all three were on their way out. My father received a tape from Charmian in which she explained how much she and the boys were missing him. They wanted him back in Australia and the effect was to plunge Dad into another state of depression, during which his thoughts returned to the possibility of giving himself up. Back in England, members of the gang were starting to qualify for parole and that was another factor for the old man to consider. He had got friendly with a young Englishman called Conti (he was of White Russian extraction and his real name was Constantine) and, as he was returning to England for Christmas in 1973, Dad decided to ask him to make discreet enquiries to see if he could find a newspaper willing to pay for the story of his return to Wandsworth Prison. Meanwhile, Raimunda returned to live in the apartment which interrupted Dad's growing friendship with a young bank clerk called Lucia.

In January 1974 Conti telephoned Dad and told him that he had met a *Daily Express* reporter, Colin Mackenzie, at a cocktail party and the upshot was that his newspaper was very keen on the story. He wanted some proof that Dad was the genuine article and, after Dad duly sent a copy of his fingerprints and signature, things moved pretty quickly. Dad was assured that only Mackenzie and Conti would be on the flight to Brazil and that only senior figures at the Express were aware of the story. On 30 January Conti phoned to say that he and Mackenzie had arrived in Rio. Dad, along with Lucia, whom he remained friendly with, went to meet them at their hotel where he was surprised to see that there were two *Express* men present – Mackenzie and Bill Lovelace. That did not please him but Lovelace, a photographer who was enchanted by Lucia's good looks, soon won him over and a deal was struck with Mackenzie for a payment of £35,000 for Dad's story, part of it to go directly to Charmian and part to Raimunda. Two days of hard work with Mackenzie's tape recorder followed and he was getting ready to leave the apartment for a third when Raimunda revealed that she might be pregnant. There was nothing unusual about that – she had been pregnant twice before and each time a friend – a nurse – had taken care of the problem. There are actually two accounts of what happened. According to my Dad, he suggested that Raimunda visit the nurse again – he didn't want this added complication, so he gave her the money for an abortion. But fate came to my rescue when Raimunda spent the money on a new outfit instead. However, according to my mum, Dad was due to make some money from an interview which he would give her for the abortion, and they would then go their separate ways.

When Dad turned up at the hotel, Lovelace was already taking bikini shots of Lucia and persuaded my father to change into a pair of swimming trunks as well for a joint picture. At the end of the photo session there was a knock at the door. Conti went to answer but was hurled backwards as it was forcefully thrown open to reveal the arrival of the police, specifically Detective Chief Superintendent Jack Slipper, head of the Flying Squad at Scotland Yard. Slipper was accompanied by another Scotland Yard policeman, Detective Inspector Peter Jones, as well as the Rio Police chief and a couple of Consular guys. Slipper said to Dad, 'Hello, Ronnie. I think you know who I am? I certainly know who you are and I'm arresting you.' Mackenzie had seemed as surprised as my Dad at the turn of events and later swore that he had no idea his bosses at the *Express* had contacted the Yard.

Dad took the view that there was no point resisting and asked Slipper not to use handcuffs on him. He wanted to make it clear that he was in the process of giving himself up anyway; that was why he was giving the interviews to Mackenzie in the first place. The party drove to Dad's apartment to pick up some clothes to take with him to England and from there went to the police headquarters where Inspector Carlos Alberto Garcia listened intently to the details of the case. Slipper was frustrated that his plans for an early exit from the country, complete with his prisoner, were scuppered by Brazilian procedures and Dad went to spend a night in prison. He shared a cell with three others who were very interested in his story. Mario, a taxi driver, suggested that a way out of my father's problem was to arrange a Brazilian child, even stealing one if necessary. The old man mentioned how only that morning Raimunda had revealed that she might be pregnant and that delighted Mario, who said that if he fathered a child in Brazil he would never be forced to leave. After another fruitless day for Slipper and Jones, any departure from Brazil was delayed for two or three days until after the weekend and Dad was permitted a visit from Raimunda. The police chief wanted to talk to her and it was clear he had some sympathy for her and my dad and that he wasn't too keen on his visitors from Scotland Yard. Raimunda said she was definitely pregnant and wanted to keep the baby whether or not Dad was forced out of Brazil. The police chief arranged for them to be filmed for a popular TV show, *Fantastico!*, which created a lot of public support for Dad.

The following day Garcia announced that my father was to be detained in Brazilian custody for ninety days pending further enquiries. Slipper and Jones returned home that night to England without their man, while controversy raged and accusations flew between Scotland Yard, the Home Office and the Foreign Office. Dad was transferred to Brasilia where there was a special prison for foreigners. On the flight he was shown a copy of the *Express* which made clear their collusion with the police and that they had no intention of paying for the story. In conversation with a federal police inspector, however, Dad learned that it was unlikely that he would be handed over to the English police because of the refusal of the British authorities to deport a number of left-wing Brazilians who had sought political asylum in Britain.

Charmian came over and, delighted as he was to see her, the atmosphere between them was obviously strained and she was upset over the fact that he was having a baby with another woman. There are three different accounts of what happened next, my Dad's version being that Charmian said she would happily divorce him if it helped him keep his freedom. She also said that were Dad to be sent to England that she would return home as well and wait for him to complete his sentence. Charmian's version, on the other hand, is that my father asked for a divorce as it would strengthen his position in Brazil. Finally, my mother's account of the whole episode is that the Brazilian Government wanted him to get a divorce, as they did not want a bigamist on their hands. Mackenzie and Raimunda became frequent visitors to the prison and, despite his reservations over the part the *Express* had played in his arrest, he agreed to Mackenzie's suggestion that they should do a book. Dad hired a lawyer who went to a family court to begin the process of confirming that he was the father of Raimunda's forthcoming child.

The ninety days were coming to an end and it was clear that the old man would not be leaving Brazil. On 6 May he was put on a plane to Rio where he was going to be released on conditional liberty. Reporters and photographers jostled for seats on the plane and a large army of newsmen waited outside the federal police headquarters following his formal release. The authorities had decided that he should be deported, but to a country that did not have an extradition treaty with the United Kingdom. He had thirty days to find somewhere that would accept him and it was clear that the unwritten ruling was that he was free to stay in Brazil. He was advised to go through the motions and see if there was a country willing to take him but newspaper inquires showed that there wasn't. Because of the news hounds massing outside the police headquarters it was agreed that Dad should wait until the morning to leave the building when hopefully the mob would have dispersed. He spent the night in the nightwatchman's room but he was too excited to sleep. Freedom felt as good then as it had when he had taken leave of Wandsworth Prison.

The press interest in my Dad was huge and Raimunda, now three months pregnant, was fast becoming something of a Brazilian celebrity. It was nice for Dad to meet up again with all the friends he had made in Brazil knowing that there was no longer any need to keep secrets from them. They all welcomed him with open arms. In time the press obsession tailed off, although Mackenzie and Lovelace stayed on waiting for Charmian's return to Brazil. She arrived on 16 May with the boys, Farley, now seven and Chris, eleven. There was a certain wariness from the children and coolness on the part of Charmian but they managed to get along and spent a lot of time in each other's company, although the conditions of Dad's release meant he had to be back home with Raimunda no later than 10 p.m.

Charmian spoke again about leaving Australia to come to Brazil to live. Her recollection is that she was ready to move to Brazil and resume a normal family life, but that my father didn't want to have the children uprooted and caused further upheaval.

After a particularly fretful night when Charmian ripped up some clothing belonging to Raimunda, she told Dad that she accepted their futures must lie apart and that she would give Dad his divorce so he was free to marry Raimunda and give the child his name. They were still in love but decided they could only be friends.

On the morning of 16 August 1974 I made my first appearance in the world, and both my parents agreed that I should be called Michael, after Mike Haynes. As Dad clapped eyes on me for the first time he remembered what the Brighton fortune teller had told him all those years ago – that he would have a child by a woman with long black hair.

4. 'I NEED MY DAD MORE THAN THE QUEEN DOES'

My earliest memories are of growing up in the fishing village of Sepetiba. When I was born we were living in my mother's small two-bedroomed flat above a bus stop on one of the busiest roads in Rio's Copacabana district, called Prado Junior. The apartment contained a double and single bed, a dining-room table, four chairs and the refrigerator in the main room. There was a tiny bathroom and even smaller kitchen. The buses in Brazil then were really noisy and cranky, and they emitted terrible fumes and thick black smoke because there were no regulations to govern them. The smoke and fumes would creep into our apartment when the window was open, and the buses were picking up passengers outside. On top of that, the tenants in the building were outnumbered by the cockroaches and rats, so it was not an ideal setting for a newborn baby. My father used his carpentry skills to brighten up the place as best he could. Friends decorated the walls by painting such things as a huge blue butterfly and a lion, because I was born under the sign of Leo. When I was four months old, Dad was sitting there one day seeing all these fumes coming into my room and he said, 'This is not right, we have got to get little Mike out of here.' A friend of my mother's told her about this pretty little fishing village about forty miles away, which would provide a peaceful setting, and so we all moved to Sepetiba.

Sometimes when I think about the way that fate has played such a big part in the lives of both my dad and me, I realise I am lucky to be here to tell the tale. I learned from Lia about how when my father first found out that my mother was pregnant, he was not certain that she wanted to keep the baby, especially as they were not really a proper couple at the time. My father had many women passing in and out of his life, and at that time Raimunda was just one of them. There was yet more drama after I was born as, when I was just two days old, I was the victim of a kidnapper. My mother was feeding me in the hospital when a man dressed as a doctor came into her room and said it was time to take me back to the nursery. But my mother had only just started feeding me, and argued with him, so in the end he just snatched me out of her arms. What the man did not know was that my grandmother was in the toilet, and when she heard my mother screaming for this man to stop she came rushing out. My grandmother started beating this man around the head with her handbag, and in the end he handed me back to my mother and ran off. What a lucky escape for me. Then when it was time for me to go home, my mother and I had to be smuggled out of the building hidden inside a laundry bin on wheels as there were hordes of photographers waiting outside the hospital to get the first pictures.

When my father had spent time in a Brazilian jail he met a tall Frenchman by the name of Fernand Legros, who was a forger. He was a good forger and would make fake necklaces and diamond rings, and even paint fake *Mona Lisas*. When he read about my birth in the newspapers he got in touch to say he would like to become my godfather. Legros suggested I should be baptised in France, and he spared no expense to turn the baptism of Mikinho, as I was known at home, into an unforgettable experience. My mother stopped off in London en route to Paris because she had arranged a deal with the *News of the World* to take pictures of the two of us outside Wandsworth Prison. This deal, and the money it made, was one of the reasons I was baptised in Europe. Once in Paris I was christened Michael Fernand Nascimento de Castro, in Notre Dame. Legros covered me with gold and diamond rings and crucifixes – all fakes. As well as having this marvellous forger for my godfather, it transpired that he had brought along the most successful porn actress in Paris at the time to be my godmother. So, my father is a train robber, my mother a stripper, my godfather a forger and my godmother a porn actress – what a fucking great start in life I had. You will notice that at that time I did not carry the surname Biggs, and this is another dramatic twist in the whole Ronnie Biggs tale. My mother had been unable to give me my father's name because he did not have any documents which proved he was indeed Ronald Arthur Biggs. Without a birth certificate, or such documents of proof, I could not be christened Michael Biggs. Had the British Government known this, they could have applied for my father to come home right there and then, so it was kept a big secret and only my mother and Lia Pickston

– Johnny's wife – knew. (Johnny Pickston was a fellow 'Englishman abroad'. My father hit it off with Johnny straight away after settling in Rio, running into him outside a bank. They became lifelong friends.) It was not until I was nine years of age, that the Supreme Court of Brazil gave me the right to alter my birth certificate and properly change my name to Michael Fernand Nascimento de Castro Biggs, thanks to Lia who managed to get my father a social security number and legal documents lasting two years.

The whole trip to Europe for my christening blew my mother's mind and she became totally seduced by the idea of Paris and Europe, seeing what a life she could have and how much money she could earn for herself. Legros encouraged her by offering her a place to stay, so when we got back to Brazil she broke the news to my dad that she was going to live in Europe. She softened the blow by saying she would send lots of money back home to support my father and me. My dad did not try to stop her; he could see her mind was made up. There was also the fact that there was a big cultural difference between the two of them; my Dad was an Englishman who had seen half the world, while my mum was a poor half-Indian girl who, until she was five and had her first proper dress, walked around in flour bags. On my mother's side, my grandmother was Indian, and my grandfather was a mixture of French black, so mix that with my dad who was English and you had a DNA gang bang!

My mother was always a distant figure to me, and to a certain extent she still is. Our relationship is one whereby we are friends; we are very open with each other and can talk to each other about anything and everything. I know my mum talks to me about things in her life which she wouldn't discuss with my brothers. But then again, she knows I am the only son she has got who won't give a fuck about anything – I could shock her far more easily with my stories than she could shock me with hers. When I have told her things in the past she has said, 'Jesus Christ! Did you really do that? I was afraid of doing that when I was your age.' But I would say, 'Yes, I did it, and I liked doing it. As a matter of fact I wouldn't mind doing it again!' So it is a very open relationship, although very distant. In many ways I don't really know my mum, and she doesn't really know me. We are good friends, but she is more like a sister or a cousin than a mother figure. I love my mother, but because she was away for so much of my early life there is no real maternal bond. She doesn't influence the decisions in my life; I don't have the same feelings for her as I do for my dad.

I was very annoyed with my mother recently as, when I brought my father back to Britain, she sold her story to a newspaper without talking to me first. She was proud of the money she got, but in reality I could have earned her three times the amount if she had just bothered to call me. My mum was born under the sign of Leo and she will do whatever she wants to do. Once she gets an idea in her head she will do it without bothering to discuss it with anyone. When my dad went into hospital she came to London again and signed an agreement with another newspaper promising them pictures of the two of us. Yet she didn't know I had already signed a deal with a rival paper, and so I had to step in and change her deal for her, although I still salvaged some money for her. I had to tell her the least she could do in future was give me the courtesy of a call.

So for the second time in his life Ronnie Biggs settled down to raise a family. Again, using his carpentry skills, my father turned our two-floor house in Sepetiba into a beautiful home. The whole garden was filled with sand, and there were all kinds of trees growing there, with lots of fruit. It was at this time that my father started experimenting with drugs. He used 'puff' but one day my mother came home with some cow manure for her tomatoes, and the next thing we knew there were magic mushrooms growing among the tomatoes. Dad, with a few friends, went through the lot of them. My mum left for Europe soon after and it was just the two of us. We didn't have much money but we were happy. I remember how the old man built me my first bed, in the shape of a ship, with different-coloured lights which blinked at night. As well as building me toys he did odd carpentry jobs for the neighbours and that gave us enough money to get by. It was a lovely place in which to grow up; the beach was five minutes away, and there was a park opposite the house.

After a few years my father put me into my first school, and it was then that I first noticed my dad was different to other parents. When the other fathers or mothers came to collect their children they would be dressed for work, but my dad was always wearing shorts and flip-flops, without a shirt, his long hair and huge sideburns standing out. I realised my dad was different. With my mother away, my father had been introduced to a woman by the name of Ursula – or Ulla – Sopher, a mother of three young children, and they became friends and eventually lovers. My father was not much of a letter writer, so he did not communicate very often with my mother, which annoyed her because she wanted to know how I was getting on. She also found out about Ulla, and she stopped sending my father money. Christmas came and it was a bleak time for us. We had an account with the corner shop and every time my father went in there for some bread or milk he got a filthy look from the owner as if to say, 'When are you going to pay me?' So that particular Christmas it was just my father and me; we couldn't even afford a turkey for dinner, but we had a great time. Out of the blue there was fresh interest in his story when a television company from Argentina turned up on our doorstep. Once word got out that we were in Sepetiba we were visited by other crews from Germany, Japan, Belgium and Australia, and soon my dad had enough money to pay off his debts – including money he had borrowed from Ulla.

My dad used to take the bus into town to sign in or pick up supplies and most of the time he would take me with him. But on occasions it was easier for him to go alone, so he would leave me in the care of our neighbours. They had a son aged about thirteen, and this fucker started molesting me. I was only three years old at the time. When his mum said it was time for Mike to take a shower, he stepped in and said he would give me a shower. He would have his hands all over me, while masturbating, although thankfully he never actually sexually assaulted me. One day when my dad was giving me a shower I turned to him and asked, 'Aren't you going to have a wank then, Dad?' When he asked me what I was talking about I explained to him what the thirteen-year-old neighbour did. The old man was ready to kill this boy, so he had a word with his father and said, 'If I ever see your son getting close to my son, I shall go to jail, because I am going to kill your son.' They didn't know if my dad was a heavy or not and, even though they did not want to believe it of their son, the threat was enough for them to send him away to live with family in another state, and our relations with these neighbours were cut. Some years later I found out that the boy molested another child and was actually killed in an act of revenge.

There were other people living in our house by this time, because the old man had turned it into a bit of a hippy community, with people visiting from all over the world and staying for a few weeks. One of the colourful characters I remember was a mad German photographer called Armin Heim. One night my dad rushed out of his room, yelling to Armin that he was being attacked by a giant spider. Armin charged into the room with a stick and a knife to confront this giant spider, but it turned out to be a baby bat with a broken wing – Dad was a little spaced out. Armin nursed the bat like a baby until it was fit enough to fly away. Armin also had a thing about monkeys – he just loved small monkeys. He would always buy one and call it Pablo, and whenever it died he would buy another one and name it Pablo. Although the monkeys were cute creatures, they never stopped masturbating, so you would be sitting in the lounge minding your own business when this monkey would suddenly jerk off and come all over you – it was disgusting. Armin always had monkey spunk in his hair – he was mad.

There was another German living in the neighbourhood who always shouted 'God save the Queen' whenever he walked past our house and saw my dad. As a joke, my dad would give a Nazi salute and shout back 'Zieg Heil'. When Armin found out about the German neighbour he went to visit him, and it turned out that he really was a Nazi on the run, who showed Armin all his swastikas and army knives. Some of the hippies in the house wanted to tell the authorities about the Nazi, but my dad thought it would be safer to leave well alone, as he didn't want the Nazi network taking revenge against me.

Outside our house was a huge fruit tree that I loved to climb. My father would always tell me not to do it, and would say, 'Mikey, you mustn't climb that tree because you will fall off and hurt yourself.' But when you are just a young child you don't listen to those kind of parental warnings, and my response was always, 'Of course I won't.' But one day I was really high up and one of the branches snapped. I came falling down, hitting everything in sight, and I lost consciousness because I hit my head on the way down. I also suffered a nasty gash on my right arm. On that day, Johnny Pickston decided to pay my dad a visit, and as he arrived outside the house he saw me dangling from the tree, out cold and covered in blood. Johnny picked me up and as I came round he helped me out of the tree. At that point my dad came running out and he was fuming, and I could hear him screaming, 'I told him, I told him, I told him.' It is strange what goes through a child's mind, because all I could think was, 'Great! I have had an accident so I won't have to go to school,' especially as the gash on my arm was quite a bad one. Johnny was telling my dad that I needed to be taken to the hospital and stitched up, but he was having none of it. My dad wanted me to learn a lesson, so his attitude was, 'He'll be all right, we'll put a few Band-Aids on him and send him to school.' That was lesson number one – always listen to what your dad has got to say! I went to school covered in cuts and bruises, and the headmaster was shocked by my appearance. But my dad assured him I was OK and said the most that would happen is that I would have a scar on my arm. He was dead right, because I have the scar to this day as a permanent reminder.

In April 1977 a squadron of British warships arrived in Rio's dockland area of Praca Maua to take part in some naval exercises with the Brazilian fleet, and it was at this time that I first came to realise my dad had stolen something. My dad bumped into some of the sailors and, when they discovered he was the legendary Ronnie Biggs, they invited him aboard their ship, the HMS *Danae*, to meet the rest of the lads, some of whom were big fans of his. My dad sat on board drinking warm beer, duty-free of course, and signing autographs, and was a big hit with the sailors. Once word got out that Ronnie Biggs was on board, my father had to make a hasty exit, because the Admiralty did not want the embarrassment, but news of his visit to the fleet made headlines in the press anyway. When I saw the reporters questioning my dad, I got it into my young head that he had stolen a ship – my dad was a ship robber and it sounded like a big adventure to me. He was always trying to tell me he had stolen something, but I didn't realise what it was. He was also always telling me that I shouldn't be too proud of him because what he did was wrong. He always made a point of telling me he had made a mistake, but he also told me he had been unfairly sentenced. He always believed criminals should go to jail, and had his sentence not been so excessive he would have served his time and not escaped.

It was while we were living in Sepetiba that in February 1978 the Sex Pistols came to Brazil. The group had fallen out during a tour of America and Johnny Rotten, the singer, and Sid Vicious, who played bass, decided to quit the group. Malcolm McLaren, the group's manager, came to Brazil with the two remaining members of the group, Steve Jones who played guitar, and drummer Paul Cook. McLaren saw a chance for publicity by attempting to reform the Pistols in Rio with two of the most wanted men in the world, my father and Martin Bormann, a Nazi war criminal. McLaren contacted my father but was unable to get hold of Bormann, so he hired an actor who stood in for Bormann dressed in uniform and jackboots. During his time with McLaren, my father told him he reckoned he could write a song in a similar vein to the band's famous anthems, and so he wrote a piece called 'A Punk Prayer', which he recorded with Jones and Cook in a Rio studio. The song was later released under the title 'No One Is Innocent' and sold more than seven million copies around the world. He also appeared as a member of the gang in a film they made entitled *The Great Rock 'n' Roll Swindle*. So the Pistols hung out with Ronnie Biggs while in Brazil. I don't remember the faces but I remember a lot of people in our house, a lot of drinking and a lot of women. There was also a lot of what I called 'English tobacco' being smoked. My dad has always been a non-smoker, but he smoked 'English tobacco' which was his code name for dope. You don't tell your kids that you smoke dope, so he told me he smoked 'English tobacco' and I could see that the guys from the Sex Pistols were smoking it too. I remember these great parties at the house, with everyone off their head and dancing around naked. It was like the hippy days in Brazil with lots of free love.

The old man was always very open with me about sex, and I knew the facts of life from an early age. My father caught me more than once with a copy of one of his *Playboy* magazines in my hands, trying to put my dick into one of the girls in the picture, and he used to joke about the fact that I was shagging all his *Playboy* magazines.

Although I was only four at the time, I have clear memories of the first attempt to kidnap my father, which happened in April 1979. The kidnappers claimed to be a second-unit film crew who were in Rio to film fill-in shots for *Moonraker*, which had recently been filmed there. They befriended my father by offering him a part in a future film they were making, with big financial incentives to entice him. All the time they were also trying to win me over, so they promised me walkie-talkies and bought me Coca-colas and toys. One day my dad went to sign in at the federal police station and he said to me, 'Mike, you are going to have to hold your tongue because we are going to have to stay here for a few hours.' I didn't know what was going on but the old man had received a tip-off from Fleet Street that a kidnap attempt would be made, so for the first time in his life he did something he had never done – grassed people up. The federal police building is very grim and grey, with steel doors, and tables and chairs made of steel and covered with a plastic made to look like leather. It smells of mildew and even at a young age I could feel a very heavy karma inside, as many people were tortured and killed there during the repression years. It is a place I have always hated and still do. Dad told the federal police that there were a couple of men standing outside waiting for him to come out. This was on a Thursday. Dad had to sign in twice a week – on Tuesdays and Thursdays – and their plan was to kidnap him on a Thursday after he had signed in so that it would be five days before the Brazilian police missed him. So once the federal police knew about it they started arresting everyone. The kidnappers had invited my father to lunch at the Copacabana Palace, but my dad sent Johnny Pickston and his son Kevin, Armin the mad German, and four other friends to meet them instead and have a freebie lunch. The seven of them ordered all the most expensive food and drink, such as lobster and champagne, and really went to town at the kidnappers' expense. When they looked at the menu they didn't look at the food, they looked at the prices. After sitting at the police station for a few hours an officer came in and said they had arrested one of the kidnappers. They rounded up the rest and sent them off in their own plane. The chief of police, a man named Barradas, turned to them and said, 'If you want Biggs, you come and talk to me, don't try anything until you talk to me.'

After the first kidnap attempt Ulla told my dad she didn't want us living out in Sepetiba. By this time she was in love with my father, and he was happy to have found someone who spoke English, and who he could talk to on his level because Ulla had been educated in Switzerland and America. They could sit down and talk about Darwin, or play Scrabble, or cards, which is something he could not do with my mother. So we moved into Ulla's house. Ulla had three children from a previous marriage, and the father of those children used to refer to my father as 'the assassin', and said he did not want 'the assassin and his little bastard kid' around his children, Carla, Felipe and Alex. Ulla stood up to him, however, and put up with a lot to get us to live in her house. My father couldn't help with the bills, so he fixed up the place instead, taking off the doors and sanding and varnishing them, then painting the whole place. Carla was the little princess and Felipe was a bookworm, who later went on to become a computer buff, but my favourite was Alex. He was the eldest son, a musician, and he was the hippy of the trio, playing bass and smoking dope with my dad. When he was thirteen he had a seventeen-year-old girlfriend and Ulla used to allow him to have sex with her under her roof, as she was very open-minded. Alex wanted to go to the United States to study music and had secured a scholarship at the Berkeley School of Music in Boston, but his businessman father was having none of it and refused to finance him. However, my father was on Alex's side and because he had recently earned some money from his own ventures with television companies, he stepped in and loaned Alex the money, telling him to pay him back whenever he could. I think Alex was still paying him off twenty years later. My father was just happy to have helped this kid, and he even made him a case for his huge bass guitar; but the old man didn't want to make a proper case with all the curves, so he made him a box which looked like a coffin. I think it made quite an impression when Alex arrived at New York airport. Alex has still got the box to this day – it was so well made.

I was sent to a Catholic school run by nuns. They took a shine to the bastard son of the train robber and were very kind to me and taught me to read and write. These were happy times for about two years, until Ulla and my father decided things were not working out between them and they could no longer live together. My dad knew an English woman called Margaret who lived in Rio but who was returning home to visit her family for six months, and he asked if we could live in her place while she was away. In return, my dad offered to do up her house for her, with his carpentry and decorating skills, which she readily agreed to. Margaret's maid had gone away but she put us in touch with her sister, Rosa, and she became our maid. I hated Rosa from the first moment I met her, and told my father I did not want that woman looking after us, but nobody was going to listen to a five-year-old. We lived there for six months and then carried on moving around, staying in various flats or friends' apartments, with my dad doing them up to pay our way, and by now Rosa was part of our family, and came with us. I had stopped hating her and couldn't imagine our family without her. We eventually found a luxurious apartment on the eighteenth floor of a tall yellow building called the Apollo, overlooking the bay of Guanabara, Sugar Loaf Mountain and Botafogo beach. The view was amazing over Guanabara and it meant a lot to the old man because that was the picture-postcard scene which had taken him to Rio in the first place all those years ago when he was in hiding in Australia.

I had to go to a new school, again a Catholic one, but as soon as I walked in I was dubbed the son of the thief. I was beaten up by the other kids on a regular basis; even the teachers didn't like me, and I hated the place with a passion. I did not tell my father or anyone else I was getting beaten up, but one day when Rosa picked me up I bent down to tie up my shoe lace and another kid ran up and punched me in the back. I fell down and when I got back up Rosa glared at me and said, 'If you do not go back and beat the shit out of that kid, I am going to scrape your face against the wall.' I looked at the wall which was full of jagged edges and knew that was going to hurt, so I opted to run back into the school after this other kid, frightened that, if I didn't beat him up then, Rosa was going to give me a painful lesson. I chased the kid into the toilets and started beating him up. I thought to myself, 'Wow, I can do this, I can actually hit somebody.'

I looked behind me and saw that Rosa had followed me in and was standing at the door of the toilets watching me beat him up. I went over to Rosa and said, 'I did it, I beat him up,' and she said, 'Good boy, now we must go and tell your father – and you are not going to take shit from anyone else ever again.' From then on, I thought, maybe other kids can go home with scratches and bruises instead of me. I knew the bullies would still come after me, but at least I was ready for them.

My father was becoming more involved in The Biggs Experience, meeting tourists, so at the beginning of 1981 he decided that, as well as Rosa the maid, we needed a nanny to keep an eye on me. He hired a pretty Brazilian mulatto girl in her early twenties by the name of Zelia. One night I woke up thirsty, so I walked through the living room to go to the kitchen for a drink; I came across my dad lying flat on his back on the settee having a puff, with my nanny bouncing up and down on top of him, having sex. I said, 'Dad, I'm thirsty,' and he got really pissed off because I was interrupting his session with the nanny. He gave me a drink of water, but by then my mind was fixed on the thought of my father fucking my nanny, and I thought, 'If he is fucking my nanny, I want to fuck her too!' After that I was always trying to grab Zelia's tits and in the end she gave in and let me play with them. I was touching her all over and trying to imitate my dad.

Our lives were to change dramatically again on 16 March of that year. Johnny Pickston had been due to meet my father for drinks that evening, but my father never showed up. It was out of character for my father to let down Johnny without calling him and when Johnny couldn't find him he went home and called our apartment. Zelia had not heard from my father either and became frightened when Johnny called, so he came to our apartment to take care of me. The next morning Zelia woke me up and said, 'Mike, your Dad's not home, he didn't come back to the house last night.' Zelia was already in love with my father and she was upset, so I tried to calm her down. I said that maybe he got drunk last night and stayed at a friend's house, or maybe he was with another woman, but she said he would have called to let us know – he wouldn't leave me without calling. I still wasn't terribly concerned because I did not know at the time that my father had again been subject to a kidnap attempt – this time successfully – but I had confidence in Johnny and said to him, 'You will help me find my father, Uncle John. I know you will help find him for me, he did not come home to put me asleep last night.' Johnny Pickston knew something was wrong but he reassuringly told me, 'We will find your father, Mike.' Then after informing the federal police of my father's disappearance he took me back to his house so that he and his wife Lia could look after me. It was then that I suddenly had four concerned women fighting over me – Lia, my mother, Ulla and Charmian.

My mother had heard the news of my father's kidnapping and so she decided to fly to Brazil and take me back to live with her in Switzerland. In her eyes, it looked as if Ron would be gone for a long time and I would be left in Brazil without any parents. Lia knew that if my mother came and took me, there would be no chance of my father ever returning to Brazil; the only hope was for me to stay in Brazil and appeal for his return. On the morning my mother was due to fly into Rio, Lia asked her lawyer, Dr Dayse Teixeira, to go with us to the Juvenile Court at 7 a.m. and ask the Juvenile Judge, Dr Craveiro de Almeida, to grant Lia and Johnny Pickston legal custody of me as their foster child. Lia had even woken up the judge in the middle of the night to warn him that we would be coming, and she told him to prepare himself! Then we arrived at the courthouse half an hour before it opened and waited on the steps. Lia appealed to the judge by saying, 'If you do not grant us custody then you are taking away this boy's only hope of seeing his father again. His dad is all he knows, and he mustn't be handed over to a mother he has seen only once in his life.' The judge saw things our way and agreed to pass my guardianship over to Lia, but there were still some cunning tactics which needed to be employed if we were going to foil my mother's attempts to take me back. My mother was flying in with a lawyer and would be heading straight for the courthouse, because she had the right to take me away with her. So we needed to stall her until all the fostering papers for Lia and Johnny had been signed and sealed. The judge was on our side, and he got one of the clerks to lead my mother to a room in the courthouse to face the media while our legal papers were processed. It gave us a half hour head start and by the time she was ready to make her claim for me, it was too late, Lia and Johnny were my legal foster parents. I remember that I was shown into the room where my mum was waiting, and it was a very difficult situation for me. I hadn't seen her since I was a few years younger, so she was just an image in my head rather than a person, a scent, or a voice. But here she was, and the way she looked was influenced by her Swiss lifestyle, so she wore a shiny bright yellow outfit and big European-style glasses. I was frightened because I really didn't know this woman who wanted to take me away to Switzerland. Flash guns from the media cameras started popping and my mum was frantic; she grabbed me, trying to protect me from the press. She was clutching me around the neck, and I was grabbing the arm of a sofa to try and pull myself away. To highlight the fact that my mother didn't really know me, she had brought some chocolate for me but, unlike most children, that is the one thing I really hated, and I still cannot touch it. Lia then came in and told her she was now my legal guardian and my mum was both distraught and furious at the same time. A few years later I asked my mum why she was so keen to take me away, and she told me that because there was such a lack of communication, she didn't know that by taking me out of Brazil it would have harmed my father's chances of returning. Had Lia explained to her that I needed to stay in Brazil in order for my father to come back, then she would have dropped her claim willingly. After beating off my mother, Lia had two other battles to fight. Ulla came forward and said that as she had been my father's companion for the past five years, including us all living together for two years, she thought I should live with her until my father came home, because I knew her and trusted her. On top of that, Australian newspapers then reported that Charmian claimed she wanted to look after Ron's boy, and Lia was furious. But it turned out that Charmian had made no such claim – it was just a story invented by the Aussie media. At least my father's other lover, Zelia, did not try to claim me, and she did the decent thing by leaving me with people she trusted. She also handed over my birth certificate to Lia, because she had seen it in our house and knew the authorities mustn't see it, otherwise they would find out that Ronnie Biggs was not legally registered as my father. Not knowing any of this, I had decided that I wanted to stay with Lia and Johnny, but only because they were far less strict than Ulla. Lia couldn't do enough for me, and Johnny was a great laugh to be with.

Life was a bit of a circus because once the press had learned about the kidnap we had photographers camped outside the building and in apartments opposite, with their cameras permanently trained on our windows trying to take pictures of me. The same gang who had tried to kidnap my father two years earlier had struck again and this time they had been successful. Everybody knew what had happened to Ronnie Biggs except for me, and I was just told that my dad had gone travelling to São Paulo, which was another state. Johnny was very positive throughout this whole period and whenever we talked he would say, 'When your father comes back ...' rather than, '*If* your father comes back ...' I enjoyed living with the Pickstons, but I was also concerned about my dad, so Johnny tried to keep me entertained. He was an actor and a playwright so he said to me, 'Let's rehearse a show to put on for when your father comes back.' It was called *An Old Tyme Music Hall* and we spent hours dressing up, singing, dancing, telling jokes, tipping our hats and pointing our canes, and it was great fun.

In the middle of this chaos, our lives were altered once again. In Rio there was a weekly children's television programme and a young rookie reporter from TV Globo by the name of Gloria Maria was in the neighbourhood looking for children to take part in a vox pop for a new toy which had come on to the market. When she arrived at the apartment block where the Pickstons lived she asked the porter if there were any children inside. He told her that Mike Biggs, the son of the kidnapped train robber, was upstairs on the ninth floor and she seized her chance. When Lia discovered that Gloria was not one of the 'pack' and was simply there filming for a children's programme, she made her an offer she couldn't refuse. Lia told Gloria that if she filmed me the way her and Johnny wanted her to, then she would be the only reporter any of us would talk to and therefore get all the Biggs exclusives. Gloria knew this was her big break; outside you had the world's media yet here she was given special access to Michael Biggs, so she was determined not to let down Lia. Gloria filmed me and Johnny rehearsing our show – the very first public performance of *An Old Tyme Music Hall* with Mike and 'Uncle John' – and then she had the first interview with me. It was a difficult interview for Gloria because I still didn't know my father had been kidnapped, so she had to ask me questions in such a way as not to let the cat out of the bag and traumatise me. She was relatively new in the job and this was her first proper interview, and it was to prove one hell of a big break for her. Subconsciously I had been prepped for the interview by Johnny, who told me to be careful what I said, as this could help get my dad back, and he told me just to tell the people that my father was more important to me than to the British Government. So I went in front of the camera and said, 'I know the Queen needs my father, but I need him a lot more,' and it came across so pure and innocent. When the interview was later screened on prime-time television it was seen by the wife of Mr Abi-Ackel, the Brazilian Minister of Justice, plus the wife of the president, and it touched their hearts and those of many other women throughout Brazil. They thought, 'This poor kid, his mother is not here, his father has been kidnapped and he is living with this other couple; this is not right.' That is when the wife of the Minister of Justice turned to her husband and told him, 'We have got to get that kid's father back to Brazil.' If you are the country's Minister of Justice you don't need your wife ringing you at the office every day asking, 'What are you doing to get that boy's father back?' She was talking to other ministers' wives, so you had all these tough military generals who ruled Brazil with an iron fist being nagged by their wives to get my father back, and they knew they had to act. One evening Mr Abi-Ackel appeared on the TV news speaking from the Brasilia Dawn Palace and he said, 'Hello Mike, hello Mr and Mrs Pickston; you won. We will bring Ronald Biggs back home. We love you Mike, you know your rights as a Brazilian citizen. Good luck to you Mike.' The legal team working on dad's case found a loophole in the Barbadian constitution, and the next thing I knew, my father was on the telephone, and Johnny was shouting, 'Your dad's coming home!' TV Globo had a camera crew in the apartment at the time and filmed us talking, and my dad broke down on the other end of the phone. I was saying, 'Dad, I can't hear you, I can't hear you,' and he couldn't speak because he was crying. He said, 'Listen Mike, I can't talk, but I'll be there tomorrow, I'll be with you.' Finally there was an end to all this.

Lia took me shopping and bought a new set of clothes for me so that I looked my best for when my dad came home, and the next day we set off for the airport. It was mayhem, with a convoy of media vehicles chasing and following us, with cameramen hanging out of the windows taking photographs of all of us. At least some of my dad's burly friends accompanied us to protect us, and when we got to the airport I was pushed through the crowd to wait at the arrival doors. In those days the glass was transparent, and I was banging on it waiting for my father. All of a sudden, the glass shattered, and people thought I had done it by banging my fists, when really the force of the crowd pushing and shoving had made it crack. So we were moved to another door and then I saw my dad appear. My heart was racing and when the door opened I just raced to him and jumped into his arms. Carl Lewis wouldn't have got near me! We were both in tears and I asked him a question which has stuck with us ever since, 'Dad, why do people cry when they are happy?' He just held me tight. Many of the photographers had missed me running to my dad, and they shouted for me to run to him again, so they could get the images this time. I didn't want to let go of my dad, but he realised that we had to play ball for the media and he told me to do as they asked. My dad held me again and then he gave Johnny Pickston a beautiful hug as if to say, 'Thanks mate for looking after my boy.' My dad put me on his shoulders and we forced our way through the crowd, with me shouting, 'Get back, leave my dad alone!' Outside the airport, Armin was waiting with his sports car. He took my father and me in his car while Lia and Johnny went in a separate one, and we were speeding along towards the Pickstons' apartment with the press chasing us again. My father kept saying, 'Armin, slow down, I have just had my neck saved and I don't need to die like this.' Despite Armin's efforts, Lia and Johnny arrived only seconds after us. Lia opened a way through the waiting media by wildly waving her handbag and bashing anybody within reach – it was a hilarious sight – until we finally got inside. I was alone with my father in my bedroom and he broke down, hugging me and not sure what to say. But I said, 'It's OK Dad, it's over now.'

We all spent the night together and then the next day we moved back to our apartment in Botafogo. I had missed forty days of school, but my father sent me back to the same Catholic school I hated. Suddenly I was a celebrity and all the teachers who had been horrible to me because I was the train robber's son were nice and polite to me, but I still despised every minute of my time there. I also got abuse from the kids, and I became a fighter again because I wouldn't take any shit from anybody. I owe a huge debt of thanks to Johnny and Lia for all they did for me while my dad was away. Lia tried to give my guardianship back to my father but she couldn't because he didn't have any documents. She kicked up such a fuss and went all the way to the Supreme Court of Justice to plead for my right to be given my father's name. They ruled in our favour and my father was given a social security number and ID documents valid for two years.

My father had actually come close to securing his own identity card a year before the kidnapping, but he had an unsavoury meeting with the federal police after a fascinating character by the name of Albert Spagiarri, the thief who tunnelled under the main road to rob the Bank of Nice, came to Rio. Spagiarri's crime was carried out without guns, without violence and without hatred, and he wrote those words in a message that he left on the wall of the vault, along with the well-known symbol for the CND. He was caught but managed to escape and made his way to South America where he became known as France's answer to Ronnie Biggs. In 1980 *Paris Match* was in Brazil and they wanted to film Spagiarri and my father together. They met in an apartment near Colombus, and Spagiarri was a master of disguise, so he was wearing a false moustache and Afro wig. The idea was that Spagiarri would interview my father, who would pretend not to know who was doing the interview. Spagiarri asked my father, 'What would you do, Mr Biggs, if you met Albert Spagiarri?' To which my father replied, 'Who is Albert Spagiarri?' The interviewer said, 'He, Mr Biggs, is the most famous runaway in the world.' But my dad grinned at him and said, 'Sorry pal, but you are looking at the most famous runaway in the world.' Spagiarri was in no position to argue. I was six years old at the time and I remember that Spagiarri was very nice to me, leaving me his moustache and wig as a reminder.

When news came out that my father had met Spagiarri, the federal police came to see my old man and asked for the address of the building where the two of them had met. But my dad had been on the booze all day, and he'd had a few puffs, so he genuinely couldn't remember the address of the apartment. The police thought my father was covering up, but he just couldn't pinpoint which building it was. The chief of police pulled out an identity card, which was the one thing my father had never had in Brazil and which he wanted, and said, 'You are just delaying this even more.' He showed my dad the actual identity card, which was ready and waiting for Ronnie Biggs should the Brazilian government ever decide to give it to him. Then he threw the card back into a drawer and dismissed my dad. My dad tried to find the building, as Spagiarri had left the country by then, but he just couldn't remember where it was.

After the kidnapping, interest in the whole Ronnie Biggs story picked up again and my dad was making money from interviews and tourists, which meant we could survive. But the follow-up to Gloria's interview was now around the next corner, which began one day when we got a visit from the heads of CBS Records in Brazil. The executives were headed by a a couple of guys, Marco Maynardanda Spaniard called Tomas Munoz, who was president of the company at the time. He had seen my television appeal for my father and decided I had exactly what it took to front a child band. They had already recruited another boy, eight-year-old Toby, and a girl named Simony who was five, from a talent show on television and both of them could sing like birds, but they wanted me to anchor the trio, which was to be called 'A Turma do Balao Magico', or 'The Magic Balloon Gang'. I was sitting on the floor playing with my train set when my dad turned to me and said, 'Mike, would you like to sing in a band?' I said, 'Sure, why not?' and I was in. They asked me what I wanted to sing and I said, '"Oh, Susanna".' The next thing I knew, I was taken to a recording studio to record a version of 'Oh, Susanna' which was written for us. That was the launch of The Magic Balloon Gang, and we were to prove to be an overnight success.

5. THE MAGIC BALLOON GANG

It was not until after I recorded my version of 'Oh, Susanna' that I was introduced to the other two children in The Magic Balloon Gang, when the three of us were called together for our first photo shoot. My dad had gone out and bought me new clothes for the occasion, and I wore a shirt with a bright orange tie – thanks, Dad! Simony's two front teeth were missing, so she gave a gappy smile as she sat there holding a doll. Toby was the eldest child and he was holding a kite, as if flying it, against a false countryside background. This was the picture for our first album, with a hundred small hot-air balloons and a clown behind us – all very appealing for young children. Toby and Simony were good singers, which is why they had been chosen for the band, whereas I was there because of who I was and the way I could talk. In all the interviews, I was the one up there talking my lungs off, proclaiming that we were the biggest band in Brazil and we were going to sell out wherever we played, while the other two were a bit shy and stayed in the background. It even got to the point where Simony's mother, Maria, gave her a hard time and said, 'Mike is always the one talking; you should get in front of the camera and make sure you do some of the talking – don't let him do it all.'

Toby's father was a taxi driver in São Paulo and his mother a housewife, but his older brothers were musicians who taught him how to sing at a very early age, and he could sing like a bird. His mother, Dona Rosa, would take him to child talent shows and he also did modelling, because he was a very good-looking kid. Simony's family were gypsies, hard-core circus people. Her granddad ran the circus and was also the lion tamer, and all the relatives were the acrobats and trapeze artists. It was a traditional circus and I had a lot of respect for them and for the hard work they put in. The one problem was that they were very greedy. They lived on a very poor estate with eight of them living in one tiny apartment, but when Simony got her first pay cheque her mother went out and bought the most expensive car in the country, the XR3, which had just been launched in Brazil. It was a status symbol because suddenly their lives had changed, but it was perhaps not the best thing to be driving on such a poor estate, and needless to say within 24 hours someone had put a couple of bullets in her husband and took the car away, and he nearly died. Both Toby and Simony had been spotted by CBS on the Raul Gil talent show, which was screened on one of the smaller channels, and both were great singers.

CBS had already appointed a manager for the band, a very capable young Brazilian woman called Monica Neves. She was married to the head of EMI Records and was also the niece of the next President of Brazil, and under Monica things ran very smoothly. She wanted to take things slowly, with us doing a few shows in the regions. There had been entertainment shows for young children before, but something like The Magic Balloon Gang was unheard of when we first arrived on the scene. It was the first time you had kids performing for kids, and we were singing innocent songs. The parents who brought their children along to our shows looked at this eight-year-old and two six-year-olds and thought, 'Ah, how cute.' We started doing our shows on a platform on the back of a truck. It was very rural as our bus would pull into some park, the truck and the sound system would already be set up, and we would get up there on stage and perform for about a hundred kids, with a rodeo going on at the side. Everything was on playback, so we just danced around and mimed, and we had a lot of fun. Before long we started playing at The Playcentre in São Paulo, which was Brazil's answer to Disney's Epcot Centre, and very popular with children. The theme park hired us to do six shows a weekend – three on Saturday and three on Sunday – each one lasting 45 minutes. We had clowns and lots of other characters in our show. One of our songs was about a really skinny chicken who laid a lot of eggs, so we had a woman dressed up as a chicken who came on when we performed that particular song. Then when we sang 'Oh, Susanna' we came in on wooden horses, dressed as cowboys with plastic pistols; it was very well received. We were really good, as if born for the stage. Our contract with The Playcentre was for six months and after the first weekend of shows Monica went to my father and gave him a large bundle of money. He was impressed and he asked her, 'Is this for the whole six months?' When she told him that no, it was for one weekend, he was gobsmacked. He said, 'What, all of that!' She told him, 'Ron, don't worry, there is plenty more where that came from.'

After working for The Playcentre we went south, right on the border between Brazil and Uruguay. It was the first time I had ever been in a jumbo jet, and I was amazed. I thought it was the start of my pop-star life, although once we arrived we were taken to a crappy hotel. We were asked to perform in a sports gymnasium and the place was packed. It was mind-blowing because we thought, 'Wow, all these people are looking at us.' To be honest, I wasn't interested in singing at all at the time – singing for me was a waste of time. I loved playing on stage, doing the act. I was the worst singer in the band but I was the most active, and also the one who people saw as the scamp. I would dance more than the others and climb up the speakers, giving it the young rock-star bit!

Through all these appearances in front of crowds of children, The Magic Balloon Gang were taking off and, after recording our first album, CBS immediately started work on our second one. One of the tracks on the second album was called 'Superfantastico' and on it we were joined by one of Brazil's top recording artists, Djavan. He was already a Brazilian icon, but working with us boosted his career even more. 'Superfantastico' was a catchy tune which became a great favourite with the public and it was the song we used to wind up our shows. The record went through the roof, earning The Magic Balloon Gang our first platinum disc. I don't think even CBS believed it would be that big. I'll never forget the day I heard 'Superfantastico' on the radio for the first time, because we were suddenly producing music for adults and it was being played on every radio station across the country. From then on our concerts were attracting a minimum of 5,000 children wherever we went, and as we became bigger it meant our second-class hotels were replaced by deluxe accommodation when we were on tour. Monica also signed a deal with the Brazilian air force whereby we advertised for them in return for a private plane. This became vital because by road it would have taken several hours to reach certain states.

The contract with CBS allowed for one parent to accompany each child, and my father received permission from the federal police to travel with me. By then, he had been signing in twice a week for six years, and – apart from the time he was kidnapped – he'd never missed a day, so they felt they could trust him because they knew his movements were genuine. If he couldn't make it on the day he was supposed to sign in, he simply told the police where he would be and went to sign on another day, taking his airline ticket to prove where he had been. They knew my dad was no danger to anyone and was trying to live a normal life. I think that by then they felt it was also a waste of paper, having Ronnie Biggs turn up twice a week to sign his name – there must be thousands of copies of his signatures stored away somewhere in Rio.

At this point, TV Globo came on the scene. They saw our popularity and decided to do a breakfast-time programme called Magic Balloon, which was almost – but not quite – a rip-off of our name. From what I heard at the time, Simony's mother persuaded TV Globo that her daughter should present the show on her own, and that she didn't need the boys. Of course this meant more money for Simony and less for the rest of us. Simony started presenting it on her own and this angered my father and Toby's parents. I didn't really care one way or the other. We were making what seemed to my ten-year-old self bucket-loads of money, paying all the bills, and were even thinking of buying our own house. Dad didn't need to do his own interviews or meet tourists and tell the Ronnie Biggs story, he could live off the money I was making and could concentrate on being my father. As more money came in, we moved from apartment to apartment, going up in size and standard as we went along. Life was moving at a rapid pace. Simony was on the television programme five days a week and we were doing more concerts than we could handle. Before long there was a public outcry over the Magic Balloon show. The public wanted to know why it was only Simony on the programme, and where were Toby and I? The public's reaction was strong enough to persuade TV Globo to add Toby and me to the show, but Simony's mother started demanding a bigger slice of the profits because she had got the contract with TV Globo, and because Simony was the only girl in the band. Monica disagreed and felt all profits from the band should be split evenly, so Simony's mother appointed her own agent for her daughter, a very greedy man named Paulo

Ricardo. He gave Monica a hard time asking for accounts of everything involving the band, right down to the number of paper clips she used! Monica warned CBS that they would have a serious problem if they did not get Simony out of the band at that point, but our second album was doing well and they did not want to jeopardise things. However, the friction continued.

We were asked to record an opening trailer for the television special. They wanted us inside a hot-air balloon enjoying ourselves, so they hired Brazil's most famous hot-air balloonist, a guy named Truffi, to take us up, and they had three helicopters around us doing the filming. Truffi and his wife were in the balloon with us but they had to crouch down so they were out of the camera shot. However, the helicopters flew too close to the balloon and the downdraft created by their rotor-blades caused the balloon to plummet downwards. Truffi grabbed his radio and desperately waved his arms and shouted at the top of his voice for the helicopters to pull away, because he was convinced they were going to kill us. But the pilots didn't understand and thought he was telling them to follow him down. Truffi climbed on to the frame of the balloon to try and inject more hot air into it and keep us afloat, which led to people on the radio screaming, 'Get off the frame, we can see you in the shot!' The three of us were freaking out, so he told us to hold on tightly to the cylinders inside the balloon because we were going to crash. The helicopters realised they were forcing us down so they pulled away – although they carried on filming – but by then it was too late and we started hitting trees. We were all screaming and crying, and Truffi and his wife were trying to hold us and protect us. Truffi radioed the medical helicopter which was standing by and told them we were going to crash, and that headed towards us. We finally crashed into a barbed wire fence and we were all thrown out of the balloon. Toby came off worst, hitting his head hard on one of the gas cylinders. The awful changing noise his head made when it hit freaked us all out, but luckily for him it turned out he wasn't even cut. I didn't come out of it too badly. I saw the rescue helicopter arrive and ran for it, not caring what had happened to the rest of them because I was so frightened. Toby was brought on board next, and then Simony came running up, also not badly hurt. The doctors on board said the helicopter could not take any more weight, but I wasn't getting out and Toby had a big lump on his head and was crying, so we had to take off without Simony and the helicopter went back for her and Mr and Mrs Truffi. The television company wanted us to go back up to carry on filming, but there was no way our parents would let us, so they made do with the five minutes of footage which they got before we dropped out of the sky.

Not surprisingly, none of us ever wanted to fly in a balloon again, but at every concert we did it was usual for the promoters to fly us over the town a few days beforehand to promote the event. A few hundred kids below would run after us, trying to follow The Magic Balloon Gang. After the accident I remember that my dad agreed to go in the balloon instead, so you had all these kids below chasing a balloon which they thought contained Toby, Michael and Simony, when inside really was Ronnie Biggs, the Great Train Robber! My dad's hobby was photography, so he would pop his lens over the top of the balloon and take pictures of the scenes below. I have more than 3,000 pictures that he took during those trips – shots of the roofs of houses and children a hundred feet below him, waving up and smiling.

It was a happy time for my father. As I said, he didn't need to work so much; he could spend time looking after me, and he enjoyed occasionally bedding the mothers of fans who came to the concerts with their kids. We would be on tour and he would say to me, 'Why don't you sleep in Toby's room tonight, Mike?' and I would happily agree because it was fun to have a sleepover with my best mate.

By now we were household names all over Brazil. We recorded with Julio Iglesias, with Roberto Carlos – a romantic singer who was the biggest selling sensation in Brazil for fifty years, and the man after whom the Brazilian footballer was named – with Baby and Pepeu, Moraes Moreira, Leo Jaime, Metro, Djavan, Erasmo Carlos, Fabio Junior. All of these were household names in Brazil, and they all wanted to record with us. At Christmas time in Brazil the Globo network would take over the gigantic Maracana Stadium in Rio to stage a free show which was televised live to millions of homes throughout the country. The show featured acrobats, clowns and other traditional circus acts alongside show-business personalities. The arrival of Father Christmas in a helicopter marked a delirious finale. As the audience was largely made up of children, we were asked to become one of the main attractions at the 1983 show, and we had no hesitation in performing live in front of 200,000 people, plus a television audience of millions. It was nothing new for us because at this point we were used to performing to live crowds of 70,000 people in football stadia around the country. I would be getting ready to go on stage and my Dad would ask, 'Mike, tell me how it feels to perform in front of so many people.' I just said, 'Dad, it's normal, man.'

However, there were some very sad and very frightening moments when we were at the height of our popularity. Politicians would hire us to perform a concert in their region, and then advertise it free, as a way of winning votes. But the stadium might hold 35,000 people and 50,000 would turn up because it was a freebie, which led to a mad crush when the gates opened. At one venue a nine-year-old girl fell over as everyone surged in and was trampled to death as thousands of fans ran towards the stage. After that we said no more free concerts. On another occasion people tried to get to us on stage. Our security consisted of my father and two huge uncles of Simony; no-one expected us to need any more than that and I remember them sweeping us all up in their arms and running with us back to the dressing room. The police formed a human barrier, but someone reached out and grabbed my shirt and I ended up falling down the stairs leading to the dressing room and breaking my arm. I was in plaster for a month and a half. Exactly the same thing happened with Toby on a different occasion and he suffered a broken foot. When I was away from the band my dad hired an ex-policeman as my personal driver and minder, and this guy was armed. I had him with me for three and a half years, and it was embarrassing when I got invited to another kid's birthday party because I had my bouncer standing outside with a gun in his pocket.

We had a few weeks off at Christmas and my father and I headed off to a deluxe hotel in a town called Maceio in the north-east of Brazil. Christmas was a traditional family time for Ulla, so she joined us early in the New Year after spending the festive period at home. It was one of those resorts where you looked out of your bedroom window and the sea was in four different tones of blue and green, and it was beautiful to look at. We hired a beach buggy and drove across all the sand dunes in Maceio and in another nearby state called Recife. I felt a bit awkward because when we arrived in the town all the kids were after me. After signing sixty autographs you get a bit tired, but I went dune surfing with some of them, which is a bit like going on a sledge in the snow, and it was great fun. It was probably the best holiday I have had in my life. Maceio was a tiny fishing village and the only contact they had with the outside world was a television set which was housed in a cement pillar in the centre of town. There were big wooden doors which covered it when it was not in use, and a few people such as the mayor and the policeman had the keys! The whole village would gather to watch the one television. There was no electricity supply to power the set, so there were a couple of big generators which kept it going whenever it was turned on. It was a strange contrast for us because we were in a luxury hotel with electricity and all mod cons, yet this poor stretch in the centre of the village about 25 minutes drive away was without electricity. All the children would gather round the television during the day, even though the glaring sunshine made it very difficult to see the picture. Then in the evening, all the old ladies would slowly come from their houses with their fold-up chairs, and the fishermen would dress up in their nice clothes and come out too and stand there and stare at the television, with its poor reception and equally poor sound. But it didn't matter for these people – this was television for them and they just wanted to experience it. Those were images I shall never forget.

In the New Year of 1985, Monica came up with a brilliant idea. At that time in Brazil there was a famous black singer called Jair Rodrigues, who had been on the scene since the 1960s. He won the San Remo festival in Italy with his son, Jairzinho, singing a song in Italian called 'You And I'. Monica thought that it was just what The Magic Balloon Gang needed – a handsome and highly talented black child. It was brilliant marketing to bring the son of a black music icon, especially as the kid could sing, and it would appeal to the large black community in Brazil. I am disappointed to say that one of the other parents said, 'We don't want a nigger in the band,' but my dad called a meeting and explained to the others the merits of getting Jairzinho into the band.

Still some people protested, but CBS put their foot down and The Magic Balloon Gang had its fourth member, and we did our fourth album. Monica became increasingly fed up with the pressure she was being put under by Simony's mother, and she had another row about it with CBS. I had nothing against Simony's mother; I just think she wanted Simony more in the limelight, and she gave the record company an ultimatum – either Monica goes or she takes her daughter out of the band. CBS wanted to keep the band together, and Monica saw the writing on the wall. She took charge of another kids' band, The Happiness Train, and started selling them abroad. When Monica left, my father knew things would never be the same. He had a soft spot for Monica: she had been the one who looked after me if ever he couldn't go on any of the trips, and he trusted the way she handled the band. In her place we got Simony's agent, Paulo Ricardo, in charge of The Magic Balloon Gang. This was the beginning of the end for the band because Paulo didn't care if we tarnished our image in a city, because he knew we were booked up for the next ten months. If we were booked to perform somewhere for an hour and Paulo decided he wanted to leave after 45 minutes, we would leave.

There was another contributing factor in Monica's decision to walk away from the band. At this time, our television show had added a new character, Fofao. He was a doglike creature from outer space (don't ask me why!), and he joined us when we performed around the country. But Fofao had his own manager, and so the friction of three managers was too much to bear. I still didn't care too much about what was going on, because I knew I was earning more money than I could spend. But not long after Monica left, Fofao's manager had a bust-up with Paulo and split from us. Our image was suffering and, although we were still a huge attraction, promoters preferred to book a smaller band who would treat them – and their audiences – properly. And who could blame them?

My adventures with dad continued while we were on the road. We loved to go off together and explore, although we often ended up with our own little entourage. Toby's mother was very conservative, and was happy to sit in a hotel lobby and pass the time away, whereas my father and I would get out and find out what each particular town was all about. On one occasion there was a theme park in the town we were performing in, and as we had a free afternoon my father decided to take me there, rather than sit in a hotel room all day long. Toby found out where we were going and pleaded with my father to take him too; his mum trusted my dad, so she was happy for him to come along, and off we went. Toby had the equivalent of about £200 in his pocket, but my dad never let him spend a penny; he bought us burgers, ice creams, drinks, whatever we wanted. We had such a good time that at the end of it Toby turned to my dad and said, 'Mr Ronald, thank you very much, this is one of the best days of my life.' I felt sorry for Toby, even though he was older than me, because my dad was such good fun, whereas his parents were very strait-laced.

There was one great example which summed up how conservative Toby's mother was. One of the people who toured with us was a seventeen-year-old girl named Marisol, whose job it was to sell merchandise, and I fell for her in a big way, even though I was five years her junior. We used to have fun and games, and I would even sleep in her room, although she never allowed me to go all the way with her. One day, Toby's mum rang my dad in our hotel room and said, 'Mr Ronald, I need to have a serious conversation with you.' My dad thought, Oh no, what has that little prick Mike done now? Has he sworn at her, grabbed her tits, or what? Because I don't want to have to take this shit from Toby's mum. He told her he would speak to her when we all met for lunch. However, she assured him it was both private and important and asked him to visit her in her room. As my dad walked in she said to him, 'If my husband found out there was another man in my room he'd kill me.' Yet this was after we had all been working and travelling together for a few years and had become close friends. When he asked what I had done, she said, 'I saw that girl Marisol give him a full kiss on his lips!' My dad's reaction was, 'And?' But Toby's mum was shocked and she arranged for Marisol to be taken off the tour. I think my dad was just relieved because it confirmed I wasn't gay, and his reaction when he came back to the room was, 'Good on you, son.'

Another time we were appearing in the north-east and they had these fishing boats called *jangadas*. They were basically logs tied together with a sail on them – the most rustic way of sailing you could imagine. The locals would take you out into the ocean for about forty minutes until suddenly you came across a beautiful sandbank in the middle of nowhere, and you could get off and be in water up to your waist. There would be several *jangadas* in tow, some of them laden just with beer, cola and food so you could spend the whole afternoon sitting there eating and drinking. My father and I loved to get up at the crack of dawn and do all these mad things, and the others would wonder, 'What are Ron and Mike doing?' So it was no surprise when a couple of *jangadas* pulled up a little while later with the rest of the group! The old man turned to me and said, 'We'll have to start sneaking out even earlier so they don't find us.'

With just Paulo in charge now, Simony's mother brought in her whole family to work with the group. That meant there were forty people travelling with us wherever we went, and eighteen of them were from Simony's family. The people who sold the tickets were her family; the people who sold T-shirts were her family; the sound engineers were her family; the bouncers were her family; the presenter of the show was her family. So between them they were taking a huge cut. My dad warned them that we were burning our bridges, but nobody cared to listen to him.

Not only were we behaving like spoiled rock stars on-stage, but, thanks to our manager's tricks, we were disruptive off it too. I was the worst rebel of them all, and would think nothing of trashing a hotel room or a dressing room. I once got us thrown out of and barred from a top hotel because I deliberately jammed three Americans in a lift. But I blame the lifestyle I was living and the schedule I was on. I would wake up at 6.30 each morning to get ready for school. I studied in school until I was excused at midday, even though the lessons went on for another hour, and then my dad would pick me up. We'd rush off to the airport to catch the two o'clock flight to São Paulo where a car would be waiting to take us to the Globo studio. Once there we would record the following day's television show, which often meant working late into the night. Then we'd rush back to the airport to catch a flight before the last one at ten o'clock, and get home at about eleven o'clock feeling shattered. I knew all the cabin staff and pilots and I probably clocked up more air miles than most of them. I got so bored flying that I used to mark the seats on the plane, because my father and I would always have the same seat numbers. I had a little pocket knife and I would scrape a notch on the back of the seat in front so I could count how many times I'd been on that particular plane. It got to the point where there would be so many notches that my dad said, 'Don't fucking mark it any more!' I wasn't living my own life any more and I got pissed off with the whole thing.

After that first successful show in 1983, we staged a Christmas special, lasting two hours, on the last Friday before Christmas. These went on for three more years. We had a very famous Brazilian director called Mauricio Sherman in charge. In 1984, however, we worked from eleven o'clock in the morning until three o'clock the next morning because things weren't going right and the director suddenly lost his cool with me and shouted, 'You have to be professional; there are a hundred guys here working to make this show!' I blew my top and hit back, 'Fuck you, I am ten years old and I don't have to be professional. I don't want to record any more, I am walking away.' He tried to protest but my dad realised how tired I was and stepped in and said, 'One more word out of you to my kid and I'll have you. If that is how you are going to treat him I am not bringing him in for three days, so think about what you have done.' The other parents admired my dad for that because they didn't have the bottle to do it themselves, as much as they might have wanted to. But my dad didn't want to be a hero, he just wanted us kids to be shown some respect. I know it seemed a great lifestyle to my friends at school, but if only they'd known the work we put in to earn that way of life! Some days I would beg to spend a day at home playing with my toys, and the TV company would get a sweet woman to ring me up and plead with me to go into the studio. It wasn't as if we could rest at weekends, either; while all my friends were off playing football, or bumming around, we would stop recording at three o'clock on a Friday, jump on a plane to whichever city we were performing in that weekend, wake up the next morning and do some television interviews, then do the concerts. This lifestyle took its toll on all of us, and we were all overweight because we existed on a diet of hamburgers, chips and Coca-cola.

About this time a Japanese team from NTV came to Rio to make a documentary film with my father called *Long Time No See, Ronnie*, a reference to the phrase Jack Slipper was supposed to have used when he met my dad in Rio. The guys from Japan wanted to make a good impression, so they brought me a present of two brand-new Donkey Kong computer games consoles, making me probably the first person in South America to have this brand-new game which had been launched only four weeks earlier in Japan. The film they were making was to include my dad's old adversary, Slipper himself, and also me, and I was flown to Tokyo for ten days with Ulla as my chaperone. The Japanese producers were keen to make known my recording fame to their viewers and a special sleeve for The Magic Balloon Gang's latest album, *Amigos Do Pietro*, or 'Bosom Buddies', was produced for the Japanese market, with my portrait filling the back cover in place of a group shot. I remember a Brazilian newspaper writing about the documentary, and I had a laugh at my dad's expense when they asked, 'How are we going to identify the family now? Is it Mike's father, or Ronnie Biggs's son?'

When we were on the road, each parent had the option to bank at least one show each month, which meant paying the expenses but taking twice the profits. In practice, however, Paulo Ricardo and Simony's mother Monica were calling all the shots and banking the shows. However, one weekend there were three shows booked for Santa Catarina, Joinville and Blumenau, and Paulo threw down the challenge to my father to bank the shows. There was one problem with banking the shows; in the event of a show being rained off, the expenses – including the $500 per child for each show – had to be paid by whoever was doing the banking. My father decided to take the gamble, even though the shows were taking place in the far south of Brazil during the rainy season and everyone else thought he was mad. When we arrived on the Friday it was cold, grey and rainy, and it was still raining when we woke up the next morning. The first show was scheduled for 11 a.m., and it looked as though my father was facing a big loss. That was until the weather miraculously cleared up in an instant and the sun appeared. It was show time, and a good crowd turned up. The weather held out for the next two shows, making it a nice little earner for my dad, and the others congratulated him through gritted teeth. My father estimated that when Paulo came to settle up with him, he underpaid him by about $1,000. However, the old man couldn't be bothered to kick up a fuss, and in any case he felt he had a perfect response to being screwed by Paulo – he was screwing Paulo's younger sister, who was part of the troupe.

Spending so much time living the way I was with The Magic Balloon Gang meant that my schoolwork suffered, and I fell behind by more than a year. I changed schools a couple of times when we moved, and whenever I walked into a new one not only was I Mike Biggs, the son of a train robber and a stripper, I was now that boy from the band, and that didn't make my life any easier. On the one hand, when I walked into school it was nice to see all the girls look at me admiringly, but on the other hand I could see that the other boys were thinking, 'We're gonna fucking have him.' There would always be someone who would try to have a pop at me because of who I was. My only option, or so I felt, was to fight. I had been doing judo since I was six and now I decided I wanted to take up boxing, which appealed to the Englishman in my father. The first thing I did when I walked into a new school was to ask who the school bully was. My theory was simple: if I was not afraid to pick a fight with the biggest tearaway in the school, every other kid would fear me and therefore leave me alone. I was the only kid in school with an earring, I was in a band, my dad was a train robber, and I took on the school bully – nobody would want to fuck with me after that! Sometimes I looked at the bully and realised he would beat the living daylights out of me, but I had to go through with my theory. Most times I ended up being best mates with the bully because I was the only one prepared to stand up to him. However, I am not proud to say that I became a bully myself. I was a violent little kid and if somebody looked at me the wrong way I would hurt them. I knew I could fight and I knew I could punch and hurt someone. But what a prick I was. At one of the schools I was at during this time, because there was a huge mix of kids with lots of money and kids from the poorest backgrounds, there was quite a social clash. Half the kids had drivers to bring them to school while the other half didn't have enough money to eat a decent lunch. That was when I really learned how to fight, because the kids from the slums know how to have a ruck – for them it was a matter of the survival of the fittest. My dad saw that I wasn't getting a proper education, I was just being passed up the grades because they felt sorry for me, and after two years he tried to move me into a Methodist

Dad and I on the beach in Rio. Dad's up to his old tricks.

Ronnie was a Train Robber. Didn't hurt nobody!

Ulla, Dad, Fred the parrot and I. Dad looks happy and complete.

ad was an honest carpenter by trade! He found paid work on settling in Rio, nd undertook jobs until barred from working following Jack Slipper's visit.

Above Mum and Ulla together – a rare moment!

Left Mum takes a train!

Above Growing up in the shadow of a famous father.

Below Watching Dad being filmed in the TV Globo studios.

My dad's bigger than your dad!

BIGGS ELUDES YARD AGAIN!

MARIA EMILIA AMARO PICKSTON

U SOU MIKE BIGGS

40 PETALAS DE ROSAS

40 DIAS DO SEQUESTRO DE RONALD BIGGS

CRIANÇA PREDESTINADA
CRIANÇA LIBERDADE

Forty Petals of Roses – my first book! The Highway Patrol was big at the time ...

Right At a Kiss concert, displaying my own tastes in those days.

In action with the Magic Balloon Gang,
here in Rio's Maracana Stadium. At our
height we played to audiences of two
hundred thousand people.

Loving every minute of it.

Below In our backyard in Rio.

Dad and I, Irish blood.

At twenty-three.

Left Back behind bars...

Below Dad, a little the worse for wear and I, lounging. Wherever we were, if there was a stage we'd usually be up on it.

ft It became
traditional for touring
bands playing in Rio
to drop in on Ronnie
and I, and Dad loved
it because it was often
a taste of home. Here
he is with Sting, a
more welcome Police
visit than Jack
Ripper's had been!

ght Memorable
times with Wattie and
Co. from The
Exploited.

ght My favourite
ever picture of Dad.

elow On stage with
Die Toten Hosen,
complete with self-
deprecating T-shirt.

With old pal and Train-Robbery mastermind Bruce Reynolds. Coke by th pool: in reality, Dad was so happy because this was the first time he'd seen his pal face-to-face in thirty years

Dad with mate and fellow ex-pat Johnny Pickston, who looked after me while Dad was kidnapped.

With Bruce Reynold's son Nick.

The gang! *Left to right:* Bruce Reynolds, Nick and I, and Dad.

Above Thumbs up! Dad and I with Johnny.

Left Dad at his seventieth birthday party, at our flat in Rio.

Below Thank you – I'm not sure what it is but I like it! Note the poster in the background.

Above left to right: Bruce Reynolds, Roy Shaw and Dave Courtney. No prizes for guessing the topic of conversation.

Below There you go, Dad.   *Below* With my wife, Veronica.

Above That's my girl!

Left A proud grandfather. *Left to right:* Veronica, our daughter Ingrid and I, introducing Ingrid to Dad.

Left to right: me, Ingrid and Dad – three generations of Biggs!

school. But I failed the test because I was a year and a half behind the rest of the kids.

Instead he found a school for me called Eden, which was run by a bunch of refreshingly modern-minded people with hippy hearts. To become a teacher in the school you had to be a psychologist too. It was a very alternative school and the kids were sons and daughters of ex-communists, journalists, etc. You didn't have the usual kids of doctors or clerks – they came from more arty backgrounds. This school was to have a dramatic effect on my life and to this day I have a lot of affection for it, and for many of the teachers and fellow pupils I met there. It didn't start off that way, though. On my first day, as soon as I walked into the school I had a fight and I hurt this kid so badly that the headmaster called me in and told me that if one of my punches had landed a fraction higher, I would have damaged the boy's eyesight for life. I had reached the point where it wasn't fun to fight, it was fun to hurt, and that was when I realised I was going too far. I was ten years old and I couldn't handle being ridiculed for being in The Magic Balloon Gang, having them call my father an assassin and my mother a whore. I knew judo, boxing, and even kick-boxing, and this was my way of fighting back. I had become a nasty piece of work and would hurt another kid just for looking at me.

Toby had turned fourteen and he felt under a lot of pressure because people were beginning to say he was getting too old for the band, and he knew his days were numbered. We were touring at this time with a teenage band called Menudo, which featured a young Ricky Martin; we would open some concerts for them, and vice versa, depending on who was the main attraction in the particular town we were in. They were an older, sexier version of us and all the girls used to scream at them in their tight jeans, whereas I wasn't even allowed to go on stage wearing my earring – a little silver guitar. We knew one of the kids from Menudo had been replaced when he became too old for the band, so that was playing heavily on Toby's mind. My father knew we were coming to the end of our days as a group, and he made some sensible suggestions to safeguard our future. He suggested changing our television programme into a news update for kids, and also talking about social problems in it. He said we should be taught how to play musical instruments, so that in five years time I'd be playing guitar, Simony keyboards, one of the others drums, and we'd have a proper band. But I think they dismissed it as just 'the train robber's idea', so he stopped giving them ideas. CBS were getting fed up with us too, but they needed an angle to help sell our new album. They became involved in a very smart project by linking up with a bank. Anyone who bought our album would get a cheque for what would be the equivalent of £5 today, signed by the four members of The Magic Balloon Gang and you used it to open a savings account with the bank. The album sold half a million copies.

Meanwhile, the stress for Toby became too much and he developed a rare condition where his entire body became covered in spots – big, ugly ones filled with yellow pus. It was everywhere: his face, his back, even his feet, and everyone felt very sorry for him. Finally they found a new kid to replace Toby, called Ricardinho, or Little Richard, but Toby's torment wasn't over yet. We met the new kid at a photo shoot, and we tried to make him feel comfortable. But our manager decided to take Toby on tour with us so he could say a grand goodbye to the public. Every date we played was proclaimed as Toby's last concert with The Magic Balloon Gang. He would run off stage as Little Richard ran on. They would stop halfway, give each other a hug, and then carry on. This went on for eight months, four times a week, and it broke Toby's heart. The manager rubbed more salt into his wounds by paying him a smaller percentage than the rest of us, because he wasn't performing in the whole show. It wasn't just about what happened on stage, either: in our contracts we all had the right to do a solo album, but in Toby's case that was changed to a single. Toby could still sing and dance superbly, but he looked ghastly, which made the photo shoot to launch his solo career a bit of a nightmare. But he was given a good song and he was very hopeful. However, CBS knew they could not work with a kid with so much acne. They let him record the song but told him to get his own manager and promote it himself. Needless to say his mum did not know who to contact and when Toby eventually launched himself, the record flopped. Six months later, a seventeen-year-old by the name of Marquinhos Moura heard Toby's song, decided to record it himself and it went to number one in Brazil and stayed there for three months. Moura is still remembered today for that one song. That should have been Toby's glory, but I think it was his skin condition that cost him his big chance. While Toby was struggling, I was making the most of my fame by getting to meet some of the biggest bands in Brazil, such as the Mudguards Of Success, Blitz, and Urban Legion. I was a brat and I would ring up their agents and ask for tickets for their concerts, then would go and watch their shows even though I was underage. I stood on the side of the stage so I wasn't near any of the drinking areas and once, when I was at a concert of a band named Ultrage A Rigor, I was invited out front to sing with them, so I was having fun.

By now my dad and I were living in an area of Rio called Flamengo Beach. For a brief time we shared the house with an eccentric English family called the Crockers. The head of the family, Christopher Crocker, was famous for opening the first self-service restaurant in London, called The Asterix. But because he came from a family of sailors, he sold up, bought a 1910 sailing yacht without an engine or radio, and decided to take his pregnant wife to Brazil to have a Brazilian child. He wanted to sail like his old grandfather, using compasses and the stars rather than modern technology, and they did make it from England to Brazil, only they came via Africa. He became friends with my father and they found a huge place which they decided to share. While we were living with the Crockers my father bought a magnificent blue and yellow macaw named Fred. I could feel that my life wasn't ordinary, that it was exotic; I was living in a huge house, being a member of a famous kids' band, and was the son of Ronnie Biggs. Fred used to talk a lot and my father taught him lots of different words in English and Portuguese. We were still drifting a bit, though, and moved on to live in an area called the Botanical Gardens. Those days were among the happiest of my life, even though my mum decided to come and spend a month with us, which caused friction between my dad and Ulla. My mum's husband joined her and they moved into the building next door, and decided to live in Brazil, during which time my mum fell pregnant.

There was a big English community and my dad made friends with an entrepreneur in the neighbourhood named Kevin Rawlings and they became drinking partners. I befriended Kevin's stepson, Sol. As far as I was concerned, I was the next to be booted out of The

Magic Balloon Gang and I couldn't wait to be free – I'd had enough. My dad was concentrating on a few of his own business interests, although sadly he was a terrible businessman. He invested in a restaurant with my mother and also a nightclub in Copacabana with the Crockers called Crepusculo de Cubatao, which became one of the hot night spots in Rio. The club eventually ran its course and became the Kitschnet which, before closing in 1993, hosted a number of successful male strip shows for women and was Brazil's answer to the Chippendales.

In February 1984 my father heard that the apartment beneath Ulla's in Santa Teresa was up for sale. My old man used to dream about the apartment, which had a garden, because he felt he could turn it into a beautiful place. He went to look at it and although it was very run down the price was attractive, so he bought it in my name. The old man wanted to refurbish it and then present it to me as a surprise, so he brought in a team of tradesmen and labourers who began work on the renovation. We moved in a year later, when there were just a few finishing touches still needing to be done. The worm-eaten flooring had been replaced with white marble; all the old woodwork, cupboards and door frames had been burned and replaced with dark, polished hardwood; a 22 by 13-foot slate-lined swimming pool had been installed, and I had my own suite decorated in black and white, the colours of Botafogo, my favourite football team.

My father always told me he smoked English tobacco because he couldn't say he was a puffer. Once when I was four he took me with him to sign in at the Federal Police and one of the officers offered him a cigarette. I intervened and said, 'No, officer, my dad doesn't want that because he doesn't smoke cigarettes, he smokes only English tobacco.' The policeman laughed it off because he didn't understand, while my old man thought to himself, Thank Christ I didn't tell Mike I smoked dope! Now it was the end of 1985 and I was at a stage in my life where I was about to discover what English tobacco really was. I could smell it from my dad's room, and I could also smell it from the kids who smoked it in the street at night. Then I went to a few parties and my friends would say, 'Look at those kids, they are smoking dope!' I suddenly thought, Hey, wait a minute, I recognise that smell because I smell it three times a day in my house – it's English tobacco.

One day I walked into my dad's bedroom and there was a big bag of dope on top of the television. I was fiddling with it when my dad came in and I confronted him and asked, 'What's this?' He was a bit sheepish and said, 'I don't know, it belongs to Paulo, the housekeeper, but it isn't mine.' Paulo Garcia was someone who had performed with The Magic Balloon Gang, dressing up and acting out all our songs, and when the band finished he came to work for us because he became a good friend of the family. But I was wise to my father and blew my top and said, 'Dad, it's yours, and it isn't English tobacco, it's marijuana – and you can go to jail for this! How can you take this risk, bringing drugs into the house?' All this from an eleven-year-old brat, giving my dad a hard time, but he knew I had a point. I complained to my dad and to Ulla for five days solid, until Ulla had enough of me. She took me into my dad's room, rolled a joint and said, 'Right, you are going to smoke this and after that you can give us a hard time about it. Once you know what you are talking about you can call us drug users or whatever, but until you know what marijuana is I am not going to allow you to talk to your father and me like this.' As I lit the joint my father walked in and asked, 'What the fuck is going on?' Ulla just gave him a mean glare as if to say 'don't get involved' and he turned around and walked back out. After smoking the joint I immediately fell asleep and did not wake up until the next morning, and I started shouting, 'That stuff is bollocks, it doesn't do anything for you.' I just thought, What a waste of time, you smoke that shit and you go to sleep, nothing else happens. My dad said, 'Hey man, getting stoned is not about laughing and falling on the floor, it is about turning the lights off, putting some good music on and listening to it.' I smoked a few more joints but every time I just ended up falling asleep, so I couldn't see what all the fuss was about. About six months later my older half-brother Chris visited from Australia with a few of his mates, all of whom were in their early twenties, for a six-month tour of South America. My dad cleared out the lounge and put bunk beds in so they could all stay with us. These guys were into shagging birds, smoking dope and listening to music. The 1986 World Cup finals were on in Mexico and one day I sat down with my brother and his friends to watch Brazil play Poland in the second phase. They were rolling joints before the game, and I told

them I had been smoking that stuff on and off for the past six months
and it did nothing but send me to sleep, but I decided to watch the
game with them and smoke a joint at the same time. Brazil won 4-0
and all I can say is, what a fucking football game that was! The grass
had never looked so green and the ball had never looked so round,
and when Brazil scored I went berserk. I suddenly saw the appeal of
my joint. I was twelve years old, still at school, still in The Magic
Balloon Gang, listening to Led Zeppelin, Pink Floyd, The Beatles, and
smoking dope.

By now all three of us in the band were fed up with the whole Magic
Balloon thing. We were fed up with each other, we were fed up
signing autographs, and we were fed up performing. I remember we
appeared at a show house in Rio called The Scala and the critics
slaughtered us. They said we didn't look interested in what we were
doing – which was right – and that our fake microphones didn't even
have wires attached to them to make them look real. People were still
paying good money to see us, so they were entitled at least to see us
try to pretend we were singing; but we weren't even bothering to do
that. I was tired and I didn't give a fuck any more. Our television
programme was getting bad ratings now, and things were not helped
by the fact that we were chubby, unhealthy looking kids. I was also
stoned out of my box most of the time, because I used to pinch my
old man's roaches and take them on tour with me. One time I was
about to go on-stage and I had forgotten to take out my earring, so the
manager stopped me and told me to remove it. I was so stoned I just
said to him, 'Fuck you,' and he said, 'Don't talk to me like that, kid; I
don't have to take this shit from you.' So I said, 'Fuck you, if I don't
go on stage with my earring, then I don't go on stage at all.' My hair
was quite long at the time and the earring was a tiny silver guitar, so
I didn't think it would even be seen, so I stood my ground. I just sat
on the staircase and said, 'Go on, start the show without me, see if I
give a fuck. I have had enough of this band anyway.' In the end, he
gave in and I went on stage wearing my earring. I had shagged my first
bird by this time so I felt more than able to stand up to him.

Discovering marijuana was one thing but, as I said, I had also
discovered sex. There were still workmen in the house when we

moved in and one afternoon one of them decided to finish early. I heard him tell the others, 'Fuck it, I fancy going to a whorehouse.' I went up to him and said, 'Take me with you.' He told me not to be silly but I said, 'Come on man, I am twelve, I want to fuck a woman, I should be fucking women by now.' I nagged him so much that he eventually said, 'Fuck it, if someone is going to break this kid in, I may as well.' The next thing I knew, I was in a whorehouse with three women licking my whole body. The most any of my mates had done at the age of twelve was snog a girl, and here I was getting a blow job and tits in my mouth and having a good time. When I got home that evening my dad was furious because one of the other workmen had told him where I'd been, and he warned me that if I ever messed with a whore again he would 'beat the fuck' out of me. He gave me the freedom to bring girls to the house if I wanted to, as well as smoking dope and having the occasional beer, but he did not want me to go behind his back and do things which broke his trust. Half of me was hurt and remorseful because I had betrayed my dad, but the other half was celebrating because I'd just shagged three women in one day and I felt like Superman with an eight-foot long dick! My father also told the man who had taken me to the whorehouse never to come near me again, and sacked him from the decorating team.

A lot of people will condemn my dad for letting me do the things I did at home; but, had I not been allowed to smoke dope in the house at an early age, I think I would have been doing drugs behind his back in the streets. At least he knew where I was and what I was doing. And I might have been tempted then to try something harder. He made a point of hiding his gear, but I always found it; I would go through his wardrobe, check his clothes and shoes, look under the bed, inside his typewriter; it was cat and mouse but I would always find his roaches or his puff. I used to smoke in the bathroom on the band's bus and then return to my seat at the back, and when my father saw me looking red-eyed and spaced out he would give me a hard time in English so the others didn't understand what was going on. He was furious, and rightly so. He allowed me to smoke at home because he wanted to be able to control what I did and keep it under his own roof. But he knew I was not like any normal twelve-year-old – I had been exposed to a lot of things most people don't get to see in an entire lifetime. After one concert my dad took me to one side and told me I looked pathetic on-stage. I was forgetting my lines and stopping in the middle of the show and standing there staring upwards. In the end he stopped travelling with me, and that gave me the freedom to have sex with the sixteen-year-old groupies, because there were always plenty around.

I was spared Toby's treatment of being replaced in the group by someone younger because CBS finally had enough, and after nearly six years and five albums they pulled the plug on the whole Magic Balloon Gang. But we were hired by a Brazilian record label called Som Livre, or Free Sounds, which belonged to the Globo network, and we recorded our sixth and final album. We all had to dress as clowns for the publicity shots, and I had to pose with my fingers in my ears and sticking out my tongue, as if to say 'nah-nah-nah-nah-nah' which meant I was again the target of the Mickey-takers at school, and that pissed me off. Our concerts were no longer playing to 70,000 people, and we were lucky to attract 7,000. We were looking tired and fed up and the ratings for our television show were sliding too, so Globo said they didn't want us any more. There had been rivalry on the show between Simony and us boys. We all used to receive fan mail, and we discovered that she had started ripping up some of ours. It was three to one, and we decided that every letter we found addressed to Simony we would hide. In the studio there was a gap behind one of the pieces of scenery, and we hid all Simony's fan mail behind there. This went on for ages; it was our game, and it got to the point where there were a couple of thousand letters there. One day Simony found out and she went for me. She lunged at me with her long nails, screaming, 'You bastard.' I slapped her back, and one of the make-up artists got in between us. All hell broke loose. Simony's family came rushing out and were shouting, 'See, that's what you get from the son of a thief and the son of a whore.' Rosa was with me that day and she shouted back, 'Don't say those things, his father's mistakes are not his mistakes.' Life is funny the way it works out, because only a year ago Simony fell pregnant by a rap artist in Brazil who was also a convicted armed robber. I thought there was a certain irony that this girl who once called me the son of a thief, ended up living with a convicted armed robber and having his baby. When I told my dad this, after he'd had his second stroke, he fell about laughing. But I know how tough she had it when she was younger, so I wish her all the luck in the world.

Channel Six, an alternative smaller television station, wanted to hire us for a show, but the director was Sherman, the man I'd been unable to get along with. He messed us around again so my father told him to get lost and we walked out. That was the last we heard of him, although he is still famous in Brazil today. He was a nice enough guy, he just didn't know how to handle children. There was another great director at the time named Paulo Neto, and he was the opposite of Sherman. If we worked a full day and were tired, he would rather call us back the next day irrespective of the cost of the film crew, because he knew how important it was to have us looking fresh-faced and happy. Finally, we did a concert and 3,000 people turned up, and we knew that was the end. The Magic Balloon Gang was officially disbanded, but we'd had a good run and sold hundreds of thousands of records.

The others accepted the fact that our time was up, although Little Richard took it the hardest because he had been in the band the shortest period and been involved in only two albums. I was over the moon – I didn't have to do any more concerts; I could wear my earring; I could get stoned; I could fuck as many girls as I liked; I could travel. Freedom came into my life and there is one day I shall never forget, shortly after The Magic Balloon Gang ended when I was thirteen. I woke up one morning, had a puff, and then shaved my head so that nobody would recognise me. Then I put on a baseball cap and for the first time in my life I caught the bus to school all by myself. I was actually going somewhere by myself – no armed security surrounding me, and no daddy holding my hand. That bus ride is something I shall remember for the rest of my life. I caught the 572 bus, and I sat there listening to the Beatles on my Walkman, with nobody pointing at me. I finally had the freedom I'd been craving. But I was thirteen, a teenager; and now the real madness started in my life.

6. SUMMER OF THE CAN

All teenagers have it hard, but I became weird. I'd left the Magic Balloon Gang, and was enjoying my new-found freedom, but was suddenly very insecure. Still at least half a year behind the other kids at school, I was having private lessons to try and keep up, but these made me miserable. A lot of women were coming on to me, but I never knew if they wanted to be with me because I was a nice guy, or because of the person I'd been. For a year or so, I went only with women who were nineteen and older, because I was a bit too advanced for girls my own age. I could have conversations with these older girls which no boys my age could have, because I had seen and done so much and had so many stories to tell. I was still at the same school and I quite liked it, especially as the staff had a good way of dealing with the rebel students. If you skipped a class because you preferred to sit on the patio strumming your guitar then the headmaster would come up to you and say, 'Hey man, you have got to go to class. If not, I shall send a note to your parents telling them, because they are working hard to pay for you to come here. It is up to you, if you want to be a bum and then have to repeat the year with the younger kids, it's up to you, but if you want to play guitar then you may as well leave now and go and do it on the street.' I respected that approach because it made it the student's responsibility – they'd feel stupid and so return to class.

The best times for me of course were the weekends and school holidays, and I had the perfect holiday retreat. Shortly before The Magic Balloon Gang had folded, my mother had returned to Brazil, pregnant and married to a Swiss bank clerk called Gerard. At first they went to live with my grandparents in the north of the country, but when their son Andre was born they came back to Rio. Gerard was supposed to be a good cook, and my mother persuaded my father to go into partnership with them and open up a restaurant in a lovely little beach town called Buzios. Buzios had been put on the map by Brigitte Bardot, the French film star. She first went there for a holiday in the 1960s, and the tiny fishing village grew into a sophisticated weekend getaway for Rio's 'beautiful people', who arrived to take advantage of the peninsula's nineteen beaches during the day, and its abundance of bars and restaurants in the evening. It was Rio's answer to St Tropez in the South of France. My father took a team of builders to give the restaurant a facelift and stocked the cellar with a good selection of wines. During one of my many visits to Buzios I met a guy who had a sailing yacht and we became friends. He chartered the boat for trips and told me he needed some help, and offered me the chance to work with him and learn all about sailing. I took him up on his offer and the two of us would take all the tourists on trips. I took to the tasks like a duck to water and really developed a passion for sailing. I did not enjoy staying with my mum because she was very strict and had lots of rules for me – things I had never adhered to before – so I asked if I could stay on the boat, and that became my home when I was in Buzios. It also gave me somewhere to take girls for a shag and a smoke!

Unfortunately for my mother and father, competition with the restaurant was strong and customers were too few and far between. Gerard, as chef, found himself with little to do except drink our best wine and eventually the restaurant went bust and we all lost a lot of money in the venture. I still went to Buzios at any opportunity to enjoy myself on the beach and continue my passion for sailing. During this time I met a 29-year-old Brazilian woman named Margaret; she'd been married to a millionaire but they'd separated, so she lived on her own in the town. She took a shine to me and invited me to stay at her house rather than on the boat, and I moved in with her. We had a little fling, although we did not go all the way and have intercourse. My mum got very pissed off when I moved in with Margaret, telling me I was only a kid. But I told her to get lost, because I'd made my own money and felt I was free to do as I pleased.

My mother got fed up with Buzios and decided to move back to Rio, where she wanted to take a tourism course and become a tour guide. She had also become estranged from Gerard after the restaurant flopped. However, she had nowhere to stay so she moved into our house. It meant I had to share my bedroom with my mother, my baby brother, and his nanny; then my grandmother came down from the north-east and she stayed in my room as well. I had always been on my own, so losing my privacy drove me mad. I couldn't even have a wank in my room, let alone smoke dope or take a girl back there. I put up with it for two months, but then I had a showdown with my dad. My dad had a word with my mum and she flipped, because she felt I was trying to kick her out of the house, whereas I only wanted her out of my room. But a solution of sorts presented itself because my mother started having a relationship with my father again. I knew my father also had another woman – a lesbian – on the side, and when his proper girlfriend Ulla found out about my mother and the lesbian, she called off the relationship, leaving my mother free to move into my father's room.

Ever since my father had met the Sex Pistols, I had taken a shine to the punk rock scene. Then one day outside school I saw a guy from the Brazilian punk movement; his was only a small group but they had all the main albums – Exploited, GBH, you name it. I got chatting to this guy and he invited me to his birthday party in a couple of days time. I really enjoyed myself and I had my hairstyle turned into a mohican, and I started hanging out with these guys. Our enemies were a group of heavy metal fans, and I was often involved in fights. It got to the point where I was attacked by a group of six kids who took my wallet, so after that I stuck drawing pins inside my new wallet so the points were sticking out, and I used it as a weapon if I was attacked; I hurt a couple of kids like that. Then one day I heard that a guy from another school, who was a couple of years older than me, was threatening to kick the shit out of me. I was not one to duck out of a fight, but I wanted to be prepared, so I raided my old man's toolkit and armed myself with a machete and a chain. I set off for the fight, but word got out to the other kid that I had a machete in my bag, and he never showed up. I went back home, dumped my schoolbag in the house and set off for a party. Unfortunately for me, my baby brother found my bag and unzipped it. My mother was standing close by and she saw Andre pull the machete out of the bag. She went mad, and when my father came home she gave him another earbashing, and heavily criticised the way he was bringing up his son. During the evening I stopped off from the party to pick up some joints to smoke, and my father was waiting for me. It was the one and only time he ever gave me a severe beating, but it was the beating of my life, with my mum standing in the background egging him on. He left my face unmarked but he punched me all over my body and threw me around the room in a bid to teach me a lesson, leaving me badly bruised. But to a large extent he knocked some sense into me, and for a while I changed my ways.

Around this time I had been hanging around with five children from a nutty family – three boys and two girls – whose mother was Irish and father Portuguese. The eldest child was seventeen and a complete tearaway. He would take his dad's car and we'd all go joyriding around the town and make a nuisance of ourselves. I loved it because I had never been a proper kid, so I was making up for lost time. But I needed something positive in which to channel my energies, and so I turned to another new passion of mine, which was ice hockey. I used to watch it on television and its physical and violent aspects suited me. There was a huge American-style shopping centre in Rio which had an ice rink, and they gave hockey lessons there, which I joined. My life consisted of going to school and then heading off to the shopping mall to skate and play ice hockey. I bought all the equipment and played for the local team, and I became quite good.

However, with my parents living as man and wife again, I couldn't stand my mother trying to control my life, so as soon as summer arrived I went back to Buzios. One thing about Buzios was that you had a lot of active drug dealers there; it had moved on from St Tropez and become more like Marbella. Whenever we went there the foreigners wanted to meet Ronald Biggs and shake his hand, so we met a lot of people from all over the world. One of the guys we met was an Irishman who was called Tyrone. This was a man who had made his money in property, but he decided to sell up and go to Brazil. He was a big guy, and a rugby player, and like my father he was a heavy drinker. At last my father had found someone who could match his ability to consume Brazilian beer, and the two of them became good friends and drinking partners. Margaret, the woman I had previously stayed with, now had a boyfriend, so I couldn't go back there, but I bumped into Tyrone when I got into Buzios and asked him if I could stay at his house. He already had some friends over from England, including a famous nightclub owner, a well-known hairdresser and another guy who was an upper-class painter and decorator, and who was the most polite one of them all. I had brought my sleeping bag with me and was happy to bunk down on the living room floor, so they let me stay. This was what became known in Brazil as 'The Summer of the Can'.

The Summer of the Can was so called because early in the summer a group of drug smugglers were sending a cargo ship full of canned tomatoes from Asia to Europe. Except that the cans did not contain tomatoes, they each contained a kilo and a half of Thai grass. However, when the ship was just off the coast of Brazil, the engine broke down and the ship began to drift towards the coast. The smugglers got cold feet, and in their panic they all abandoned the ship, leaving only the cook on board. Ironically, the innocent cook was the one who was arrested and put in prison, so he really was left to 'carry the can'. Before jumping ship, the smugglers dumped the entire cargo into the sea. The smugglers expected the cans to sink, but they floated, and the tide brought them in towards the beach. The beauty for anyone who picked up the unopened cans was that they couldn't be nicked by the *Os Homi*, 'the Man' as we called the police, because they had found the stuff floating in the sea and could claim they didn't know what was in them. All the surfers and fishermen grabbed as many cans as they could. The surfers would go into the sea to get the cans, pass them on to street kids waiting on the beach, and the street kids would run as fast as they could to people waiting in cars to ferry away this top quality Thai grass. Needless to say the price of smoke hit rock bottom that year, because it was everywhere. Tyrone bought about 750 grammes of this grass for his friends to smoke and we had a whale of a time. I was very happy; I could speak English and was among Englishmen, learning more and more about my dad's culture, and these thirty-somethings had taken a fourteen-year-old under their wing.

One night, one of the guys was walking back to the apartment after having a few beers and a smoke, when a fisherman jumped out of the bushes and offered him one of the cans of Thai grass. The fisherman wanted $50 for it, but the Englishman pulled out a £10-note and said that was all he had. The fisherman grabbed the money and handed over the can of 'tomatoes' then disappeared as quickly as he had emerged. It must have been a funny sight, because the fisherman couldn't speak English and the 'gringo' couldn't speak Portuguese, but they managed to conclude their deal. When he arrived back at the apartment, the drunk and stoned Englishman banged on the window with the can, which woke me up as I was in the living room. I went to let him in and as I opened the door he put the can in my hands and said, 'Merry Christmas!' Things didn't all go my way, though: Tyrone, the nightclub owner and the hairdresser, all came to me and said on the quiet, 'Hey Mike, do you know that the painter and decorator is trained to kill?' I was gobsmacked, and they carried on, 'Mike, we know you are into martial arts but forget your kick-boxing and all that crap, that guy can teach you something frightening.' I was stunned because he wasn't a big guy, but I naively believed them, especially as by that time I was already stoned out of my box. I asked them what it was he could do, and they said, 'Mike, he is a black belt in origami, so never upset him because his hands can kill.' I was in awe of this man, and I wanted to learn origami, as I thought it would turn me into a killer just like him. He was in on the trick, because I went upstairs to see him and asked him to teach me origami. He tried to brush me off, and said the others shouldn't have told me his secret, because nobody was supposed to know, but that just made me more determined to learn from him, so I pleaded with him to teach me. He said, 'No Mike, I can't do it. You are a young kid and if you get into a fight with another kid this will give you the power to just snap his arm, and I will feel guilty about it.' I promised him I would never use it on anyone who didn't deserve it, so he agreed to teach me this wonderful martial art called origami! He asked me if I had seen the film *The Karate Kid*, and when I told him I had he asked me if I remembered all the tasks which the boy was set in the film by his master, such as waxing his car and painting his fence. I argued with him that I wasn't going to start polishing or painting, and he said, 'Mike, that is your mistake, you need to learn patience. I am going to have to teach you the art of patience.'

He said I was ready for my first task. He gathered together the 750 grammes of Thai grass which Tyrone had bought, plus the other kilo and a half which had been bought the night before, and told me to sit down and separate the grass into three piles, the seeds, the twigs and the weed itself. For the next six days I spent six hours a day conscientiously separating the grass into the three piles, proud of the job I was doing. One afternoon I fancied a break, so I went to a nearby bar where I knew I could get a drink. There were some other teenagers in there, and I took a dislike to one of them, and an argument broke out. I said to this kid, 'Don't mess with me because I am learning origami and when I am fully trained I will hurt you badly.' Everybody in the place fell about laughing, and when they all calmed down and I managed to ask someone what all the fuss was about I discovered the true meaning of origami – the art of paper folding! I was furious and I stormed back to the house to confront the hoaxers, this fourteen-year-old kid ready to have a row with all of them. When I got back and confronted them, they just laughed, and told me to take the joke like a man, but I was angry and upset and I threatened to leave. None of them seemed to care that I was threatening to go, which only made me more depressed, so I ended up sitting down and having a smoke with them. It was a hot day and because I was the kid they asked me to go and put the Rizla papers into the fridge, to stop them from sticking together. Rizla papers were what we used to roll the joints in, but they were not available in Brazil; instead, whenever someone visited from England, they brought Rizlas with them, and we had a big box-load in the living room for all the Thai grass. I reluctantly got up to put them in the fridge, but I was still angry and wasn't concentrating on what I was doing, and I ended up putting the box of Rizlas in the freezer by mistake, which made them all stick together anyway and ruined them. I wasn't too popular after that, and I felt that was my cue to leave Buzios and return home to Santa Teresa, especially as summer was coming to an end anyway.

My father had been introduced to a Polish film director called Lech Majewski, who wanted to make a film about the life of Ronnie Biggs, entitled *Prisoner of Rio*. The cast was headed by well-known British actor Steven Berkoff, and included Paul Freeman, Peter Firth, and Brazilians José Wilker, Florinda Bolkan and Zeze Motta.

Majewski's plan was to make a true film of my father's life, and the two of them set about writing the script. They worked on it daily for two weeks and my father was very dedicated to the cause, but then Majewski decided to turn to fiction, and he introduced a kidnap plot where my father was snatched by an outraged Scotland Yard inspector, 'Jock' MacFarland, who was obsessed with getting Ronnie Biggs out of Brazil. My father lost all interest in the project at that point and left Majewski to get on with it himself. Everybody turned against Majewski, and my father formed a friendship with Berkoff, who regretted getting involved with the Pole and he said he wished he had thought of writing the screenplay and directing the film. Berkoff should have been in Brazil filming his part for three months, but the film took so long to make and went so over budget that he ended up staying for six. He went on to tell *Time Out* magazine in London, 'I myself fail to understand why people can change a perfectly good yarn for some hokum. If someone like Biggs expresses doubts about some elements of the script, then a producer who fails to listen does so at his own peril. After all, it comes from the horse's mouth. He was there.' The other unfortunate consequence was that my father fell out with Johnny Pickston. There were parts of the script, written by Majewski's wife Julia, which caused some arguments between the two of them, and they ended up having a 'sabbatical' during which they did not speak to each other for two years, and it was a hard time for both of them.

Prisoner of Rio opened at the Cannes Film Festival with a publicity scam, when the producers announced, 'Mr Biggs will be putting in a personal appearance at the festival.' There was speculation that my father was hidden aboard one of the yachts anchored off the beach, and both the press and the police gathered at the festival. The producers kept their word as Mr Biggs did put in an appearance, but it was Michael, rather than Ronnie who turned up for the premiere. The film was released in Britain at the same time as *Buster*, a film about another member of the Train Robbery gang, Buster Edwards, starring Phil Collins and Julie Walters, which rather stole the limelight from *Prisoner of Rio*. I was invited to London with my mother for the premiere of *Prisoner of Rio* in the summer of 1988 and we lived a jet-set lifestyle for a few days. This was the summer of acid, and I went clubbing and lived it up. I was invited to a show by The Mission, who had visited my father when they came to Rio, and I was introduced to a new drug, as somebody gave me my first ecstasy tablet that night. My mother did not want to return to Brazil and decided to go back to Switzerland instead, so I went home alone. It was just my dad and me in the house again, and I felt free once more. I could walk around with a joint in my mouth rather than hide away in my room, and when my mates came around to the house I didn't have my mum opening the door to them and saying, 'You guys are ruining your lives, getting stoned at fourteen years of age.'

It was about this time in my life that I realised all the lads who played guitar were shagging loads of birds. You had to do some form of art at my school, so I opted for music, especially as I reckoned the teacher was a dope smoker – hey, he had long hair! – and because a lot of good-looking girls were studying music too. I already had a guitar and I knew how to play three or four chords. I enjoyed it, because it meant I could go to parties and pull out my guitar and play a few songs – and pull a few birds. I heard that someone was selling a twelve-string guitar, which would be a huge improvement on my six-string version, but he wanted $400 for it. We were not doing too well financially, because our business ventures had struggled, and when I asked my father for the money he said he did not have it to give me just like that. However, he saw how much I wanted it and he could see I was really getting interested in music, so he went to see a German friend of his called Dieter who owned a bar in Rio. Dieter lent my father the money and told him to pay it back whenever he could, so I bought the guitar.

Life was fun again with just my father and me, and the two of us were asked to take part in a tribute concert to mark the eighth anniversary of the death of John Lennon at a place called The Flying Circus, which was a very good project for Brazilian performing artists. I became friendly with the keyboard player, an American whose name was Raymond. He had another American friend who had just bought a restaurant in a developing town forty minutes from Rio called Itaipu, which he gave a Tex-Mex theme. All his American friends who lived in the area, or who came over to stay with him, used to hang out at the restaurant, and I used to join them because I could speak

English. It was such a nice area that I spent a lot of time there during that summer, with my guitar, and the owner and his band would let me play with them in the restaurant, which had a little stage. On one particular occasion, some friends of the owner came over from America with a load of acid. It was acid paper, and the idea was that you put a piece of paper in your mouth and it would dissolve, leaving you to enjoy its effects and get high. However, the machine they used to put each drop of acid onto the paper had broken, and these guys didn't know how to wet this acid any more. They immersed all the sheets in a tub of liquid acid and then had to use tongs to pull out the sheets; then they hung all the sheets on a line, just like you do with your washing, but this had the unfortunate effect of forcing all the liquid to run down to the bottom of the sheets of paper. They had 13,000 hits of acid, but half of them were powerful from where the acid had settled on the bottom, and the other half were almost useless. It was a mess, because you couldn't be sure which was strong paper, and they lost virtually all of the money they would have made from selling the stuff. I asked them for some of the acid papers, but I must have been given the weak ones, because I tried about six and they had no effect on me. Acid was not the only new drug I tried, however. While I was spending time at the beautiful beach of Itaipuacu in the town, I bought a kayak; one day I met up with two guys who knew my father and who drove a jeep, and they agreed to help me take it to the beach on the back of their jeep. On the way we stopped off at their house and they started chopping up a line of cocaine. I had never had a line in my life and so I asked them if I could have one. As I was not quite fifteen, they refused. I told them that if they did not let me try it with them, I would go to a slum and buy some cocaine and do it on my own. If anything happened to me, I would tell my dad I did it because his mates wouldn't let me try it with them. I had them over a barrel and they relented and reluctantly gave me a line. That was my first ever snort of cocaine and it made me feel great, and very powerful. Even though I liked it, I did not do it regularly because over the years I developed a sinus problem, and that made it difficult for me.

One night one of the Americans came into the restaurant. This guy held all his sheets of acid in a plastic folder, and we all used to nag

SUMMER OF THE CAN

him for some, so he would tear off pieces and give them out. But it was weak stuff and it would only give us a light buzz. However, on this particular night, another American grabbed an entire sheet, screwed it up and put it in his mouth. As he started to chew it he got a big hit, and realised he had stumbled on something powerful. It must have been a sheet on which lots of acid had accumulated when it got soaked onto the paper. He spat it out, but another guy picked it up, tore off a piece and put it in his mouth. This guy then called me over, asked me if I wanted to find out what acid was really all about, and gave me a big piece to put in my mouth. I could feel how powerful it was and it started hitting me in a big way – I was really losing it. First of all I could feel my skin breathing, and I was scared. I didn't want the others to see how it was affecting me, so I went into the kitchen and curled up in a little area where they stored gas cylinders. I started hallucinating and I was freaking, but I had a grown-up head on my shoulders thanks to all my dad had taught me, so I told myself not to believe anything I was seeing, because I knew it would wear off in eight to ten hours and I would be OK. Raymond was in the restaurant that night and he came up to me and could see I was in trouble, although he had taken some of the acid and was badly affected by it too. He asked me if I was OK, and when I looked up at him I could see through his skin. I could see all the veins in his face and the muscles moving up and down, and then I could see the bones. It was a skeleton with long blond hair talking to me, and it was frightening. I told him to go away because I could see right through his face, and he turned to me and said, 'Goddamn it, look at your own arm.' I looked down at my arm and I could see every cell moving inside my arm. I thought 'wow!' and I sat there for ages looking at the veins and blood in my arm, watching its movement. I could literally see through my skin and I loved it – it was a great 'trip'.

After a while I felt bad. I tried to get up but I lost my balance and fell back down. I started freaking because I was unable to stand – my legs would just not support me. I then looked into a light and it blinded me; everything became silver, and I could see only the shape of people, not their faces. I had lost my balance and my vision so I called over the security guard who worked at the restaurant and said, 'Man, I am fucked. Everyone else is out of it and I have got nobody I can trust. Help me. You are the only person in here who I know has not taken acid, and you are the only person I can trust.' He helped me up and supported me, and then he walked me along the beach to a house where another one of the Americans lived. All the wives and girlfriends were in the house, and when they saw how bad I looked one of them said, 'That fucking prick, he gave a fourteen-year-old kid acid. I am going to kill him.' By now it was three o'clock in the morning, and I went and crashed out on one of the beds. A young woman came to sit with me, and she put my head on her lap and started stroking me, which made me feel better. She obviously had a soft spot for me, and she lay in bed with me and stroked my hair and my back, telling me, 'You'll be all right, don't worry.'

A few hours later my head began to clear slightly, but my vision was still fucked. Everything I looked at had bright orange and yellow circles around it, and it actually remained like that for a whole week. For a while I thought it would never return to normal and I was very frightened, but gradually it did. On that first morning after taking the huge dose of acid I decided to go for a walk on the beach, even though my legs were still wobbly. I must have looked very odd, the skinny teenager with long hair, laden with necklaces and rings, dressed in only a pair of jogging bottoms. I was still hallucinating and every time I looked up into the bright sky I could see huge butterflies with each of their wings the size of a football stadium. It was like a scene out of the film *Independence Day*, but instead of seeing flying saucers I could see butterflies. The beach of Itaipuacu was quite dangerous because it had a shelf, and as you walked into the water you could suddenly drop a metre and a half into open sea; a lot of people drowned there. Fortunately my senses told me not to go in the water, so I just lay down on the sand watching these giant butterflies flying around me. What a 'trip' I was having.

The next thing I knew, the woman who had nursed me through the night was standing above me, asking if I was OK. I told her I was cool and thanked her for saving me during the night. She told me everyone had left the house, and she took me back there and cooked me some breakfast. I spent the day there smoking dope and drinking beer, trying to avoid the sunlight. The day passed in what seemed like five minutes, and I decided I wanted to return to the beach and watch the sun set. I was sitting there watching the sun go down when the woman joined me again, and this time she had brought my sleeping bag with her from the house so that I didn't catch a chill. It got a bit cold and we climbed into the sleeping bag together to watch the sun set. The next thing I knew, this woman, who was in her late twenties, started stroking my cock, and before long we were shagging on the beach. I could see three old fishermen about a kilometre away all looking at us, and I just thought, This is wild. We stayed there all night, and my head was much clearer by the morning.

The next day I decided to go straight back to the restaurant, and I was a laughing stock when I turned up because of the way I looked. My hair was all over the place, I didn't have a shirt on, there was sand all over my body, my bare feet were black, and I was still talking with slurred speech. I sat there all day, and in the evening I just crashed out on the stage. Someone put a sheet over me because, in my absent-minded state, I'd left my sleeping bag on the beach. The next morning the same woman came looking for me, but I wanted to be left alone to play my guitar and think about the world. As far as I was concerned I had shagged this woman and wanted to move on. I had never had a steady girlfriend at that age – I had just shagged older women. It was difficult for me because I didn't identify with girls my own age. My head was still not completely clear, and it stayed that way for the next few days, as I waited for the acid to wear off. Even then, I had only to have a beer or to smoke a joint and I was out of it again.

I decided it was best for me to return home to Rio, and at the end of the week I was considering telling my father about my acid 'trip' because my eyesight was still not completely clear, but then it came back and I just got on with life without saying anything. Christmas came and we went to a big party mostly full of foreigners who didn't have family in Brazil. Ulla was there too, and she and my dad picked up their relationship again. I turned fifteen and there were new adventures awaiting me.

Smoking, sniffing or taking acid were not the only ways I could get high. There was a place a couple of hours' drive from Rio known to all the youngsters as 'Mushroom Paradise'. The fields there were inhabited by a certain type of bull, the 'Zebu', and his excrement fertilised the mushrooms. When these mushrooms were boiled and strained, they made a special tea, and if you drank the tea and waited a little while it gave you a trip. The first time I tried it, I didn't know how potent the mushroom tea was. I thought it would be like marijuana – you smoke it until it hits you. I was with a forty-year-old man who was an experienced tea drinker, and he filled an empty litre-and-a-half Coca-Cola bottle with mushroom tea. I started drinking it, but it was having no effect on me. Nobody had told me that you drink a little bit and then it takes a bit of time to start working, so I drank more and more, until in effect I had overdosed. When the magic mushroom tea began to take effect, I embarked on an awesome trip. We went for a walk in the forest and I began to feel very ill. I started hearing voices in my head saying, 'You have taken mushroom tea? So what!' The next thing I knew, I pictured myself in a giant football stadium with 120,000 people shouting 'so what!' I jumped up and shouted 'stop!' and it went away. One of the guys I was with heard me shout and came up to see if I was OK. As I looked at him, two horns sprouted from his head and he turned into the devil. I just screamed at him to get away from me, so he told me to sit down and put my feet in a little brook which we came to. As I sat there, another voice came into my head. It was the spirit of the forest and it said, 'Kid, you are in my forest and you are too stoned to be here – get the fuck out of my forest or I am going to hurt you.' I knew he meant it, and I was suddenly desperate to get out of the forest, so I asked one of the other guys to guide me out of the forest. They tried to placate me, but they could see I was freaked out, and they agreed to leave the forest with me, taking me on a route which went past a waterfall. There was a very narrow path you had to walk along to cross the waterfall, which was four metres below, and as I edged my way along it I slipped and fell. I was ahead of the others and they dared not look over the edge because they knew it was dangerous below, and they feared the worst for me. The forty-year-old man felt responsible and as he came to look for me I was getting up from the water, in between two pointed rocks. The place I fell was the only possible spot where a human body could fall and not be pierced by the rocks – I was lucky to be alive. All I had were two scratches on my body, but I was still stoned and I was giving

SUMMER OF THE CAN

myself a hard time for having got my T-shirt wet. The next morning, when my mind was back to normal, the others explained to me what had happened, so I went back to the waterfall to take a look. When I looked down and saw how lucky an escape I'd had, I just sat down and cried for about ten minutes. If there is a God, he was there protecting me that day.

On another occasion, I was staying in a house in Mushroom Paradise with a group of friends, and one of them used some of the magic mushrooms in her recipe for spaghetti Bolognese. It was one of the best meals we had, although one of the guys who didn't know about the mushrooms gave some to his dog, and we later found the poor dog hiding under the bed, having his first trip. He was shaking and cowering, but he was nursed back to normality by the girls in the house.

Then there was alcohol. Behind Eden school was a bar which all my friends and I used to go to, and the owner would sell us beer even though we were under age. There was a bottle of soft drink next to our glasses which was the same colour as beer, so that anyone walking past would think we were drinking that. But really our glasses contained beer. We used to call that bar 'the office'. I was arriving at school at 7.30 a.m. stoned out of my box, and at our first break three hours later I would nip round to the boozer for a beer. I was out of it most of the time. But I made some very good friends with my school mates at this time, and most of them are still my best friends today. This was the last year before the school ethos changed, and became more business-orientated, more of an elite academy for very rich kids. Now it is a highly respected school.

One night I went to a party and at four o'clock the next morning a group of us decided to move on to another boy's house where we could smoke a joint. As we were walking through the streets, I got chatting to one of the girls in the group. She told me that when I was nine, she came round to my house and got me to sign a piece of paper which said I was her boyfriend; she then went around telling all her friends that she was going out with the boy from The Magic Balloon Gang. I vaguely remembered that a girl had once come into my bedroom when I was playing with my video games, asked me to sign a piece of paper, gave me a kiss on the lips and then left – and here she was again. We got to the house and stayed together, talking and smoking dope. We ended up in one of the beds together, but nothing physical happened, we just cuddled up and went to sleep. This girl, Clarisse, was two years older than me, and she became my first steady girlfriend, someone I saw every day and went to concerts with. It was nice to be with someone more or less my own age and I learned a lot about life from her because she was great fun.

However, it didn't take me too long to make a prick of myself with Clarisse – and to make matters worse it happened on her eighteenth birthday. We were at a concert and I saw the most beautiful girl, who was the sister of one of my friends. I couldn't help myself, I was all over this other girl, and Clarisse saw me and was quite hurt. I left the concert with a friend, stoned out of my box, wondering if I would stay with Clarisse or not, and we started to walk home. The friend I left the party with, who we called LF, looked like a weirdo, but only because he had a problem with his eyes. He couldn't control them and they would roll around their sockets as if he was crazy, and he wore a pair of very thick glasses. It didn't help that he was very tall and skinny, but he was really a very nice guy. As we were walking up the very steep Santa Teresa hill we were confronted by two policemen. We both looked drunk and stoned, which of course we were, and these two particular policemen took an instant dislike to us. They could smell the dope and the alcohol on us and decided to give us a hard time. They searched us both, but luckily for us we did not have any drugs on us, as we had smoked it all at the concert, and maybe the fact they found nothing pissed them off. They told us to look them in the face, but this was impossible for my friend with the crazy eyes. One of the policemen said to him, 'I told you to fucking look at me kid!' and then he slapped him hard across his face. I couldn't believe it, and although I didn't do or say anything they noticed the expression of horror on my face. The same policeman grabbed me by my collar, pulled out his gun and shoved it into my mouth. I could feel the cold steel on my teeth and the end of the gun stretching my cheek and I was scared. He asked me if I had a problem, and I shook my head. As he pulled the gun from my mouth, I made the mistake of saying 'Why?' I was gobsmacked – I had never experienced such hostile treatment from cops before. This animal gave me a beautiful open-handed slap across my face which knocked me to the floor, and then he told me to get up. As I was getting up he could see my eyes filling with tears of anger, frustration, and also a feeling of helplessness. They slapped us both once more and told us that if they ever saw us again they would take us in, and then they just left, leaving us shaken and hurt – both mentally and physically. I felt for my friend; I had tears rolling down my cheeks and I could see pools of tears welling up on the bottom of his thick glasses. We both remained silent for the rest of the fifteen-minute walk up the hill, but we had a sense of brotherhood. Our night had changed dramatically. We had started off our walk as two teenagers laughing and talking, debating whether I would stay with my girlfriend or move on to this other sexy girl, then all of a sudden the spirit had been knocked out of us in my first hard encounter with the Brazilian police.

Rio can be a dangerous city, and on another occasion I found myself caught up in a shoot-out. I was walking home from the pub one afternoon when two guys on a motorbike came tearing past me and screeched to a halt. The one riding pillion was shouting, 'It's no use, there's nowhere to run!' Then he pulled out a gun. Across the road was a bar, and a guy who was sitting having a beer saw what was going on and pulled out a gun of his own. Suddenly, for no reason at all, a gunfight broke out in broad daylight. I was stunned and stood rooted to the spot, until I heard a bullet whistle past my head and quickly I dived for cover under a parked car. I lay there listening to guns banging and women screaming until suddenly the motorbike sped away and the police arrived. When I heard the police I climbed out from underneath the car, but one of the cops thought I was part of the gunfight and pointed his gun at me. As he came over he saw I was just a long-haired hippy in flip-flops and a flower-power shirt. He asked me what I was doing but I could hardly speak from shock. People were lying dead or injured on the pavement and an ambulance was arriving, and then I looked at the car under which I had been hiding and saw it had been hit with bullets, which freaked me even more. The policeman saw the state I was in and said, 'Kid, get the fuck out of here.' But as I started to walk away he called me back and asked if I would recognise the shooters on the motorbike if I saw them again. I suddenly sobered up, thought for a moment and then shook my head. I said, 'I could not recognise anyone.' He gave me a mean look but he understood my position, and he said, 'OK kid, go home to your mother.'

Two of my best school friends, Joanna and Gabriella, were half-sisters who lived in a fantastic sixteenth-century-style castle at the top of a hill in Rio, with a magnificent view of the city. Their parents were sculptors and they had been commissioned to go to Europe for a project, leaving the two girls behind with the freedom of the castle. I slept with these girls on a regular basis, but we were such close friends that we never touched each other – we were just mates and did not want to spoil a beautiful friendship. While their parents were away I went to their home every day after school, and we had lots of wild parties. I still had a sheet of acid which I had brought home from Itaipu and I ended up giving pieces of it to the other kids who came to the parties. During one of the parties I met a thirteen-year-old girl named Marie and dated her for about five weeks, having great sex with her despite us both being under age. She got bored with me after a while, but she had a very cute best friend called Mia who liked to imitate everything she did. That included sleeping with the same boys, so I moved on from Marie and went out with Mia instead. I really fell for this girl in a big way and thought she was the one I would spend the rest of my life with. She was also thirteen and had no thoughts about settling down or getting serious, so after a few weeks she told me she wanted to see other boys, which left me feeling devastated – even though I was sleeping with other girls behind her back whenever the opportunity arose. But when I heard that she had started sleeping with someone else, I felt shattered. One day when I went to the castle I was introduced to Guga, a boy who was a year older than me. He didn't know who I was, but I realised immediately that he was the one who was now shagging Mia, and so I took an instant dislike to him. That was the last thing I needed – to meet the boy who was getting it on with the girl I was still crazy about.

I tried to shrug him off but Guga turned to me and said, 'Hey, I hear you are a musician. So am I. Let's jam.' Before I knew it, he had invited himself back to my house, because he'd discovered I had a bit of puff there, plus two guitars. This was the guy I had been wanting to kill for the past few weeks, and we were now walking to my house together. On the way, he said to me, 'That castle is great isn't it? It's always full of birds, and I am fucking one of them! I have my own girlfriend, but I am fucking a cute chick called Mia just for the fun of it.' My whole world collapsed and I asked him not to carry on, and I told him I was Mia's ex-boyfriend. He was very embarrassed and apologised, because he had not realised who I was. He told me his girlfriend's name was Celine, and she was a beautiful goddess whom everyone wanted to fuck. He had Celine *and* Mia – what a bastard! We decided to go straight to the pub so I could drown my sorrows and he could bury his guilt, and between us we drank 27 bottles of beer, each one the equivalent of a pint. It turned out that he was a really nice guy, and we got on like a house on fire, so we decided to retire to my house to smoke a joint. As we were walking along he turned to me and said, 'Listen man, I know we didn't exactly get off on the right foot, but you are going to be my best mate.' I knew he was right, because we did hit it off straight away and had a lot in common, despite our differences over a certain girl. In the end it rebounded a bit on Mia, because Guga drove her mad talking about his new best friend – me – when I was the last person she needed to hear about. Finally she dumped him, and so did Celine, so I ended up having to comfort him. From then on we were inseparable. We did become best mates, and he later became my daughter's godfather. Guga's love life was back on track when he and a lovely girl, Gabriella, fell in love, and they ended up living together in one of the flats close to the castle.

Guga had been playing music since he was four, and he started teaching me a lot of what he knew. He was reading and writing music before he was reading and writing Portuguese, and he was probably the best guitar player I have ever met in my life. He now writes orchestral music. As my interest in music gathered pace, I went back to my first proper vocal teacher from my Magic Balloon days, a man named Lauro. He was an old hippy with hair down to his waist and was into the Hari Krishna movement, and he was a great teacher with an amazing voice. He was a terrific guitar player too and, as well as teaching me to sing, he improved my guitar playing. This was just about the only studying I was doing by then; when I turned sixteen, schoolwork became too stressful for me and I left Eden. Dad wouldn't let me give up altogether, so I went to a cheap college where they did evening lessons, although it was full of drop-outs.

Rod Stewart came to perform in Rio and he invited my father and me to his concert. The old man and Rod hit it off in the dressing room and when we were asked where we wanted to watch the show, we asked to sit somewhere quiet where we could have a puff without being disturbed. They put a couple of chairs on the corner of the stage behind the PA system. Rod had asked the old man what his favourite song was, to which he replied 'Sailing'. There were 35,000 people out front, but when Rod came to sing 'Sailing' he turned to the side of the stage and sang it just to my father – the audience must have wondered what the hell was going on. Rod was one of many who toured around that time, and we also got to see Big Audio Dynamite with Mick Jones, and the Happy Mondays who were very big at the time. Even former Beatle George Harrison left a note at our house saying he had stopped by for a visit, but nobody was home. My dad picked up the note, which said, 'Sorry I missed you – George' and threw it away because he didn't know who it was from. Then our neighbour came out in a flap and said, 'He was here! Beatle George was here!' And my father had just thrown away his signature.

My dad stopped being just my dad during these days, and he became my best friend as well. If I was leaving the house at midnight to go to a club, he would say, 'Oi, Michael, I'll be there with a few mates at 4 a.m. – make sure you save me a table!' It was not uncommon for me to go partying with my father. I remember one great night when we were at a party and he spent the evening chatting up a really fit bird. But then Ulla turned up unexpectedly, so he said to this woman, 'Here, have you met my son, Mike?' When my dad opened the door to my bedroom the next morning and peeked inside, he saw me asleep with that same woman beside me – it was the one that got away!

I remained in touch with my friends from Eden and I formed a band. There was Guga, me and a drummer called Ivan. A bit later on I met a thirteen-year-old hippy called Claudio who was a top pianist. He was technically brilliant and played only with older people, and he could tell them if they hit a bum note. I asked him to join our band, which we called 'Banduepa' and he said, 'Why not!' We were good and got a reputation for ourselves, and did various gigs. After a while, Guga lost a bit of interest and wanted to drop out of the band, and so I replaced him with someone else I'd met by chance on a beach. This was a nineteen-year-old called Pedro, and he was another fantastic musician. He took over from Guga and played bass guitar and composed music for us, and the band became well known and well liked on the underground scene. I was having a great time, playing my music and pulling lots of women seven or eight years older than me. One night I went to a party and Guga turned up with an ex-girlfriend I had never met before, also named Ulla, and she was beautiful and sexy. I started talking to her and there was a mutual attraction, and she started following me around; but I didn't want to pursue it any further out of respect to Guga, although he assured me they were just friends. I saw this girl a few times after that because she often came round to my house when the band was rehearsing. Then, one night, Guga rang me up and told me to call Ulla – she wanted me and was mine if I wanted her. I rang her immediately and offered to take her to the cinema because there was a film she really wanted to see. It was a really arty German film, in black and white, with Portuguese subtitles and it lasted three hours. I was so bored and I didn't appreciate the film, but at least it meant I had started dating Ulla. She was my first love and we were to stay together for four years, and I was faithful to her for the first two of those four years. It was funny because she was the ex-girlfriend of my best mate, who I had met when he was screwing my ex-girlfriend – how weird.

Religion has also played a part in my life. From a young age I have always been very interested in religion and finding out about God, and during my teens I did as much reading as I could on subjects such as Buddhism, the Christian faith, and anything else I could find. I also used to talk about religion to Rosa, who was a follower of an African religion which a lot of people know as Voodoo. But Voodoo is only the dark side of the religion, there is a whole other side to it. I started going to fortune tellers, out of interest. Some were accurate, some weren't, some were intriguing, others were a waste of time, but

I enjoyed the experience of it all and kept an open mind. Guga and his family were followers of the Camdomble – a religion which was started by slaves in Egypt 5,000 years ago – and he invited me to meet his spiritual father, Marcos, and let him throw shells for me. I went along and was both very touched and impressed by everything he told me about my life, my feelings and my desires. From then on I started following the religion as a form of relief, and I enjoyed talking to people at the meetings they held, because it is a very open form of religion whose first rule is not to criticise other religions. There would be a party for a saint and you would have *Os Homi* on one side of the room and the dealers on the other, but all weapons would be left outside. After a few years I was invited to be initiated and become a proper member of Camdomble; I was both nervous and pleased at the same time, but I decided to join, and Marcos became a dear friend as well as my spiritual father. I am not the most devout follower, but it gives me peace of mind. I once took an Australian to meet Marcos, and on the way in the car he told me how he had been having petty arguments with his girlfriend, over silly little things such as moving ashtrays. When Marcos threw his shells, he mentioned that exact same problem, using the words 'ashtrays' and the Aussie guy freaked out. I believe there are a lot of ancient cults and a lot of powers which the mind is not able to understand – how else could Uri Geller bend spoons? And I know it is no trick because I have met him several times and he has bent spoons in front of me. After my father's second stroke I was told by Marcos that my life was going to change drastically, and that I would have it hard and have to travel for a long time. He also told me a month before my father's first stroke that he should watch his health, so his words have indeed proved prophetic. But he thinks things will work out OK for me in the end.

When I reached sixteen I got my first real job. My father and I were introduced to two American guys. I thought there was something 'iffy' about these guys because they were absolutely loaded with money, and the elder of the two was married to a woman who we could clearly see was a Brazilian hooker. I found out later that the older guy was known as 'Captain America' and had been the biggest dope smuggler to the US for more than twenty years. At large for a number of years, he'd ended up living in Brazil – just like so many people on the run from the authorities! The other guy was Captain America's right-hand man, known to us as Big D. He came from a fabulously wealthy family anyway, and was married to a millionairess, but he loved the sport of smuggling dope. One day he got caught, and was facing several years in prison, but his family cut a deal with the Government. They owned thousands of acres of land in the United States, equivalent to about one third of the state they lived in, and the deal was that they gave the Government all their land in return for a light sentence for Big D. His sentence was reduced to just three years, which greatly upset the Drug Enforcement Agency who had been on his case for years and wanted to hammer him with a big sentence. Big D came to Brazil and wanted to go straight, so he bought 27 boats in the north-east of the country and set up a company importing tuna from Brazil to America. Even though the DEA knew he was going straight, they felt they still had a score to settle with him; so, whenever his fish arrived in the United States, instead of just slitting open the tuna to see if any drugs were stashed inside, they deliberately beat the tuna as much as they could, so it would be badly bruised, and the only use it had was for cat food. I knew this because I had been hired as a translator – my Dad only let me work for Big D because he knew he was 'legit' – and while I worked for him he lost three million dollars' worth of fish.

Big D was a brash American who loved going on safaris. He had a fantastic house in Buzios with a snakeskin draped across the floor of the living room, plus a zebra skin hanging from the wall, elephant tusks and various other trophies – he really was the all-American hunter. Big D was moving from Buzios into an equally splendid penthouse flat in Rio, and he said he had a job for me and another friend (an English guy who had just served five years in prison for dealing drugs and who was a bit edgy). Big D wanted us to go down to Buzios and pick up his pets. He also told us we could take along a drug dealer friend of his from Wales to help. I assumed we just had to collect Big D's pet poodle or something, have a few days in Buzios and come back to Rio, so it sounded like a sweet job. Big D trusted us all and told us to enjoy the facilities of his house for the weekend, because he was selling the place anyway. We hired a big van and the three of us set off, the Welshman carrying a lot of cocaine and hash to help pass the journey and make the weekend go with a swing. We found the house and stood outside a big wooden gate and rang the bell. All of a sudden we heard the sound of a dog's paws running towards us and it crashed into the gate at force. We'd known it was a dog, but did not realise until then that it was a female American Pit Bull Terrier, named Trixie, and she was trained to kill. Big D had sent her to a military trainer and she had been taught to go straight for the neck. Trixie was particularly edgy because she used to have a male partner, but that dog had been killed in a shoot-out.

The housekeeper came to the gate to greet us, and he was brandishing a shotgun. He locked up Trixie on the patio and let us into the house. All we were thinking was, 'How the fuck are we going to get that mad dog in the back of our van?' Once inside the house we were introduced to the other pet we were due to transport back to Rio – Joey, the twelve foot anaconda snake. We were thinking, 'Oh my God!' The Englishman started chopping up a line of coke, and he and the Irishman had a sniff. Then the three of us headed into town to find a bar and conjure up a game plan. This was on a Wednesday, and as we had no idea what we were going to do we stayed in that pub (owned by an Englishman), smoking dope and having a wild time. After three days we got a call from Big D asking us, 'Goddamn it, where are my pets?' We told him we were working on it, and he told us in no uncertain terms to make sure we were home before the weekend was up, especially as we were expected back at work on the Monday. We got back to the house on the Sunday morning and the Welshman went through his bag of drugs and found a batch of Valium, and that gave us the idea to knock out Trixie in order to get her into the van. We bought some meat and threw a piece out on to the patio for her to eat, with a Valium tablet wrapped up inside. Trixie ate it, but nothing happened to her, so we decided we needed to repeat the process and give her another Valium. Still nothing – she was not even drowsy, but just growled at us angrily. We gave her another piece of meat with two more Valium, then decided to open the patio door and see what reaction we got. Even though Trixie was a bit groggy she went for us, so we slammed the door shut, and gave her a fifth Valium. By now the housekeeper thought we were going to kill the dog, but luckily Trixie became almost motionless. That was the signal for the housekeeper to carry her to the van, and once we had her inside we tied her up to the sides of the van with ropes and sheets, so that when she came to she would not be able to move.

We still had to negotiate the snake, who was lying in a glass container, and I decided I fancied my chances with Joey. I found a hollow tube, then ripped a wire out of one of the stereo speakers, and put it through the tube and made it into a loop. I lowered the loop around the neck of the snake and pulled it very tightly – a little too tightly because the snake started choking. It reacted wildly, lashing its tail all over the place, and I freaked out. I don't know where the thought came from, especially as I was still stoned and pissed, but I screamed for the other two to get a pillowcase. By now Joey, who was still choking, was coiling his tail around the tube in a bid to snap it – or my arm. They arrived with the pillowcase just in time and I released the snake into the pillowcase and tied it up as tightly as we could. The snake bounced around the room, but we managed to lift it into the back of the van and set off immediately in the direction of Rio, drinking and puffing as we went along.

We hadn't travelled too far when, as luck would have it, we were stopped by the police. Neither of the other two had an international driver's licence and when we were told to open the glove compartment they found the cocaine and marijuana, not to mention the empty beer cans strewn across the floor. The police saw we had been drinking, taking drugs and driving, and told us we were all fucked. They arrested us and took us to the police station, which was basically just a hut on the side of the dirt road. There was only one thing to do – ask them how much they wanted to let us go. The policeman who was writing out the charges started telling us how tough his job was, and so we suggested we might be able to make life a little bit easier for him and his family. He told us he earned nearly fifty dollars a month, so the Welshman offered him two-hundred dollars, the equivalent of four months' money. As the policeman sat there pondering the offer, the Irishman also offered him two-hundred dollars. He tore up the charge sheet, gave us back our ID documents and told us to get out of there. However, our little episode with the police was not quite over. They thought we seemed a bit too eager to get on our way, so they told us to open the back of the van. Once they saw the drugged dog and the snake bouncing around in the pillow case we thought we would be in serious trouble, not just with the federal police but with the ministry for health, animals and whoever else wanted to throw the book at us. The dog was beginning to come to, and could smell the snake, which didn't help matters. As we opened the back of the van, the dog was foaming at the mouth and started growling at the policeman. The policeman turned to me, because I was the only one speaking Portuguese, and asked, 'What the fuck is this?' I simply replied, 'A madly trained American Pit Bull and a twelve-foot snake.' The policeman slammed the door shut, looked at me and said, 'Kid, get the fuck out of here now before I arrest you all – just get the fuck out of it!' We didn't need to be told twice and we carried on our journey to Rio, stopping only to roll a joint or chop a line of cocaine and have a beer. We got back to Big D's penthouse on that Sunday night and he said, 'Hell, where are my pets?' We told him they were in the back of the van and he said, 'Well don't just stand there, bring them up!' In unison the three of us said, 'Fuck you man, do it yourself!' He took them into his flat himself, and later kept them company with a baboon and an ostrich – he was that eccentric. Never had a boring Monday morning been so welcome after that weekend!

When the time came for me to leave Big D's payroll, he wanted to thank me for all my help. He had salvaged a luxury yacht which was in New Orleans being rebuilt and refurbished. The boat had already been sold to a buyer who wanted it to be delivered to the Canary Islands. So Big D offered to fly me to New Orleans, where I would join the yacht and sail to the Canaries, before flying back to Brazil – all at his expense. It sounded like a nice adventure, and with my love of boats I jumped at the chance.

The yacht was beautiful. It was about sixty feet long, with three luxury suites, Kawasaki Ninja bikes, jet skis, a fast power boat as a dinghy, a lavish dining room and bar – it was the bollocks! So it should have been really, as Big D had just sold it for three and a half million dollars. I met the rest of the crew – a captain from the Philippines, a couple of sailors from Chile and Brazil, and a Portuguese engine man who was almost completely deaf after years in noisy engine rooms. The yacht was not quite ready, as they were still putting the finishing touches to it by painting the outside and sanding the decks, so we stayed in New Orleans for a couple of weeks until we were ready to set sail. However, while having a drink with the crew one night, I learned a few stories about the boat.

It turned out that the yacht had been built in Dublin, at the same shipyard as the *Titanic*. It had even been built using the same type of steel as had been used for that ill-fated liner. The story got even freakier, because when it was first built it was taken to a lake in America and had sunk. That was when Big D salvaged it, fixed it up and sold it. When we heard this story I was not happy about crossing the Atlantic in a boat with such connections to the *Titanic*, and nor were the rest of the crew. We carried out various tests on the yacht, and everything seemed OK apart from one thing – the stabiliser tended to switch itself off and the boat would swing from side to side. We were told that the stabiliser was a new piece of equipment and this was bound to happen at least once, so we accepted it and eventually set sail for the Canaries.

A video of the yacht and its journey was being made for both Big D and the new owner, so once we were at sea the captain asked us to put out all the crystal glasses, the porcelain crockery and the silver cutlery on display in the living area, so the full luxury of the yacht could be captured on film. It was a lovely calm day, and all this went according to plan. The only problem was that the captain never asked us to put everything back in safe storage that night, and as we were all half stoned we weren't about to do it without being asked. The next day we hit the open sea and the captain announced there was a hurricane in the Gulf of Mexico, which was the route we were taking. However, it was moving away and therefore was not expected to affect our journey other than causing a bit of rough weather. Unfortunately, the hurricane suddenly switched direction and we got caught up in one almighty storm.

I had been on the high seas before, but this was a boat which quite easily could flip over and sink, and that was my main concern because these huge waves were gushing over the yacht. I went to the bridge to see the captain and he didn't really look as if he knew what he was doing, and he seemed quite afraid, so that didn't reassure me either. To make matters worse, the stabiliser decided to switch itself off again, and as soon as that happened the yacht was all over the place. I was in the main lounge and all the beautiful glasses and crockery in their display cabinets came crashing down on the floor and were smashed to pieces. As we moved forward the weather got progressively worse and suddenly there was a call from the engine room – the yacht was letting in water. In fact, the water was coming in so fast that the pumps could not cope, and before long it was knee-deep; it felt as though we were sinking. By now it was night-time and therefore dark and cold and I honestly thought I was going to die. I went to the back of the boat in the pouring rain and all I could see were the lights of oil rigs, which were miles in the distance, and I *knew* I was going to die. I don't even know a 'hail Mary' because I was never made to go to church, but I decided to make my own little prayer. I sat there in my life jacket, half stoned, and said, 'God, for fuck sake at least kill me fast, please don't let me suffer for long.' I then went back to the bridge to see what the captain was up to, and on his instrument panel I noticed a little rod with a light on it, so I asked him what it was for. He told me that the rod always had to be kept lying down, because if it was raised it sent out an SOS signal saying we were on fire, and we mustn't do that. At this time, the other crew members started hassling the captain to turn back towards New Orleans, because it was unsafe to continue further into the storm, but he argued against them. While all the commotion was happening, I thought, 'Fuck that,' and when nobody was looking I raised the emergency rod he had told me about.

Back down in the engine room, they discovered where the water gushing into the boat was coming from. It turned out that when the rudder had been fitted, it had not been bolted in properly and there was an unsealed gap letting in all the water. The engine man and another sailor both had to dive below the water – which by now was up to their waists – and tighten the bolts, coming up sporadically for air. Despite the difficult conditions they finally sealed it and the water stopped flooding in. At that point I thought I might just live, so I decided to go back to my cabin and try to get some rest. The next morning I was woken by the captain and he was furious with me. Apparently, after I sent out the distress signal, we had F15 jets flying over us to see if a fire needed to be put out. He was telling me how irresponsible I had been when his tirade was interrupted by more news from down below that one of the engines was not functioning properly because of the amount of water it had taken in. At that point, he reluctantly agreed to turn back, and I was sent to relay the good news to everyone on the boat. It took us two days to get back to the calmer waters of the Mississippi and we made it back to base at about 2 a.m. one morning. I was the first one off the boat, so I tied it to the dock at both ends, and then I ran to a public telephone and made a collect call to Brazil. My dad answered the phone and I started shouting, 'I'm alive, I'm alive!' He just said, 'What the fuck's going on, what are you talking about?' When I calmed down I told my father what had happened and then asked him to get Big D to send me an air ticket to get me back home – there was no way I was going on that cursed yacht again. In fact, the whole crew refused to go back on the boat, and Big D had to fly us all home to Brazil.

I was soon cheered up back home when one day my dad got a call saying The Rolling Stones were in town on their Voodoo Lounge Tour. They were playing at the Maracana Stadium and they wanted to meet him, so we went along to the stadium. We were taken into the Voodoo lounge, where there was a snooker table, video games and lots of food and drink. I was impressed because I had played the Maracana with The Magic Balloon Gang a few times but had never seen a backstage packed with such goodies. We were invited into the band's dressing room, and on the way we bumped into Mick Jagger. He recognised my dad instantly, but I don't think he wanted to have too much to do with him, so he just shook his hand and said it was nice to meet him. As we walked into the dressing room, we saw Keith Richards slumped on the sofa looking like a proper rock'n'roller, but as soon as he saw my old man he jumped up. My dad looked at him, stretched out his arms, and said, 'Keith . . . we're indestructible.' Keith came over and shouted, 'You're fucking right Ronnie, you're fucking right!' Then the two of them hugged as if they were old friends. Ronnie Wood got up to greet my dad too, and we could see that they were both big fans of his. Charlie Watts was the quiet one of the trio and was less animated. Keith turned to my dad and said, 'Right Ron, what do you want to drink? We've got fucking everything. We've got

Guinness here which we had shipped over, or there is champagne, wine. You name it, we've got it. If we haven't got it we'll send out for it!' The old man settled for a pint of Guinness and a joint and we all sat down and chilled out together.

After a while, Keith turned to me and said, 'I've heard that you are a musician.' I stuttered the words, 'Y-yes I am,' because this was *Keith Richards*, a hero of mine, asking if *I* was a musician. In the room was a piano and eight top quality guitars, plus some amps, for them to warm up. Keith told me to pick up one of the guitars and play him some of my Brazilian music. I have played in front of a quarter of a million people a few times, but this was the 'bottle' test – could I play to Keith Richards, one of the great guitarists of all time? As I started to play guitar, Keith sat down at the piano and joined in. What a moment in my life, jamming with Keith Richards! I felt as if my dick was twelve feet long and five feet wide! I was feeling on top of the world. When we finished, Keith said to me, 'Come on Mike, don't you want an autograph? You can show it to your kids one day.' I had been too embarrassed to ask, but he picked up a map of the Maracana Stadium and wrote on it, 'To Michael, an honorary member and a great musician.' I was so stunned that when the show started I realised I'd left the signed map in the dressing room, so I ran back to get it. However, the security guard would not let me in, so I begged him to go to the dressing room, and told him he would find the map if he did, dedicated to me. I told him how devastated I would be for the rest of my life if he didn't let me get it back, and I looked so sad that in the end I think he felt sorry for me because he escorted me backstage and let me collect my souvenir. Then I went back to the side of the stage and watched the rest of the show with my dad.

I was still going steady with Ulla who was three years older than me, and she had me wrapped around her little finger for two years. But because I had been raised only by my dad, I wasn't big on families and I didn't like meeting girls' parents. My father had always told me families were like arseholes: we all have to care for them but there is always shit coming from them. But I was serious with Ulla and had to start going to her house for lunch with her parents and on Sundays and other special occasions, which was a bit much for me. One weekend, after we had been together for two years, Ulla had to go and visit her grandparents and wanted me to go with her on the trip, but I refused, and so we rowed and she went without me. I went to a picturesque restaurant with my dad and on another table was a woman of about thirty who kept looking at me and smiling, even though I was only seventeen. She paid her bill, got up and left, but I was a bit pissed after knocking back a lot of the local firewater, so I made my excuses to my father and followed her. I caught her up and tapped her on the shoulder, and she turned around and smiled. We ended up having a mad weekend together, where I shagged her eight times in an afternoon. That triggered off a bad phase in my life when I think I had a mental problem relating to sex. I was in my prime and every woman I met I had to shag four times a night, and do it so well that she would tell her mates, and then I would shag them as well. I was still going steady with Ulla but I was fucking everything in sight, it was an obsession.

Before one New Year's Eve, 1993, Ulla and I had a fight. We were both due to spend the weekend at Guga's family farm and she went without me. But I had nowhere else to go, and all my friends had other plans, so I decided to go to the farm anyway. When I arrived Guga's mum told me there were no spare rooms, and that I would have to share with Ulla. We didn't speak to each other and Ulla took a shine to a hippy philosopher who was fifteen years older than me. Even though he wasn't particularly good looking, Ulla became attracted to his mind, and she ended up leaving me for him. This made me rebel even more and I went wild. I started having threesomes and going to orgies, and was seeing five different girls at once. All I could think of was shagging more birds, and most of the time I was having unprotected sex. When I came to my senses about eight months later I went and had my first HIV test. I knew I had slept with about a hundred women without using a condom, and the doctor told me I had to write down the name of every woman I had been with. If I couldn't remember their names I had to write down something that reminded me of them, such as where they lived or the colour of their hair. He explained that, if I had caught a disease, it would be important to try and trace it back to its origin. I worked out that in the previous twelve months alone, I had been with more than

150 different girls, which meant a new girl every three days. And that was without counting the hookers – with whom you had to wear a condom – because sometimes I just wanted to go into a whorehouse and have sex without having to take someone out to dinner first. I was a naive nineteen-year-old and I didn't think I would get Aids, and in the end I was very lucky because the test came back negative.

7. MORTALITY

My father suffered a devastating blow early in 1997 when his Ulla died. She had been having some problems with her stomach which needed an operation, but she never properly recovered and was always feeling sick, and so the old man tried to be as helpful as possible to her. One day I arrived home and there was a message on the answer phone from my father which said, 'Mike, the moment you get this message, ring me. Don't dilly-dally, don't fuck around, call me, it's very important.' I rang him immediately to ask what was wrong, and he told me Ulla had died. I was extremely upset, because I knew how much Ulla and my father cared for each other, and it was much sadder when I heard how my father had discovered her body.

The old man had gone to Ulla's flat one afternoon because he was going to be spending the night there, as he often did. They had keys to each other's homes, so he let himself in. My dad could see into Ulla's bedroom and she was lying in bed in a T-shirt with a towel wrapped around her waist. It was a warm, lazy afternoon, so my dad just assumed she had stretched out on the bed and dozed off. He decided to let her sleep, and to cook her a nice meal. He went shopping, bought all the food, some wine, and a video, so they could spend a relaxing evening together, and then went back and cooked a great meal – he was always a dab hand in the kitchen. My dad thought Ulla had been sleeping for two and a half hours, so he started to make a bit of noise in the kitchen, hoping she'd stir. When she failed to appear, he put the television on to watch the early evening news, and turned the volume up loud so it would wake her. There was still no sign of Ulla, so finally he made her a cup of tea and took it into her bedroom to wake her with it. As soon as he walked into the room he saw the legs on her pale body looked bruised, because she had been dead for a few hours. That's when he realised she wasn't asleep. My poor dad had been in the apartment for nearly three hours cooking a lovely meal and preparing for a relaxing evening, while Ulla was lying dead in the bedroom next door – it was a horrific experience for him.

I had not seen my father cry since he returned home after being kidnapped when I was five. He was incapable of crying, he was a fortress, but emotions ran high after that day. On the day Ulla died we were in her apartment and her brother suggested she should be buried as cheaply as possible. I could see my dad was furious, I could see the hatred in his eyes for this man after that comment – especially as the family were not short of money – and he stormed out of the apartment. I chased him and found him on a street corner, with his hand over his head. I asked him if he was OK and he said, 'Mike, I had to get out of there otherwise I would have kicked the shit out of that guy. How could he say that about his sister, the woman I have loved for the past twenty years?' I organised Ulla's funeral for the following day and as the coffin was being lowered into the ground my dad said, 'Goodbye Ulla.' He was about to start crying, but he held it back, so I went across to him, I hugged him, and said, 'For fuck sake Dad, cry. Please do it, do not hold it back, cry.' My dad just broke down in my arms and that was a very emotional moment for me. He was sobbing like a baby; he was being more of a human being than I had ever seen him before, in floods of tears, and I knew this would never happen again.

With the death of Ulla, weekends, too, died for my dad. For the past twenty years, since getting together with Ulla, his weekends had consisted of playing cards, having a few joints and playing snooker with her. They belonged to each other at weekends, and now his weekends were empty. They say bad luck comes in threes, and there were two other 'family' deaths in a short space of time which also upset my father. Shortly before Ulla passed away, our pet Rottweiler, Blitz, died. So I went with my dad to the local dogs' home and we picked out another baby Rottweiler – the rebel of the litter – whom we also named Blitz. We already had a dog in the family because at the age of twelve I'd bought a mini pinscher called Lua, and she took a shine to my dad; but Lua was going blind, and as Blitz began to grow he bashed Lua about. One day we put some food out for Lua but she never came when we called. I feared the worst and sure enough we found her floating dead in the pool. I pulled her out and my dad buried her in the front part of the garden. My father was so hurt, but again he couldn't cry, and he just stood there shaking his head in disbelief and said, 'What a year I am having, first we lose Blitz, then Ulla, and now Lua; what's happening here?'

My father did not talk about Ulla's death with anyone for six or seven weeks. He went on a drinking binge and would not open his heart to anyone. But one night my father never came home, and I was worried sick, wondering what had happened to him. Then I received a call from a friend of ours called Wolkmar, an Austrian guy who ran a Swiss restaurant in Rio called The Swiss House. My father had got drunk in his restaurant and Wolkmar had been kind enough to take him home with him and look after him. Wolkmar told me that my father had opened his heart to him about Ulla, and I was pleased that my dad had at last released some of the frustration inside him. I went to bed but was woken by the telephone at about 4 a.m., and this time it was my father. He said, 'Mike, I have just woken up in a dark room, and I don't know where I am. There is a bed and a telephone, but that is it, please help me. I haven't got a clue whose house I am in, but I know that I threw up because there is some vomit on my trousers.' That was so unlike my dad because he could drink a lot but never get into that state. I told him he was at Wolkmar's house, and it all came flooding back to him. He told me to go and pick him up, but I told him to fuck off because it was the early hours of the morning and I wanted to go back to bed. But he said he would be too embarrassed to face Wolkmar in the morning, and so I went and picked him up and brought him home. I think the old man realised he could no longer drink so much booze, so he started looking after himself and watching his diet – eating healthier foods and drinking less.

The next interesting invitation my father received came from the YPO, the Young Presidents' Organisation. In order to be a member, you had to be earning in excess of one million dollars a year, and you had to be under the age of forty. The YPO was having a convention in the Amazon and they wanted my dad to do a speech on crime and rehabilitation. I went with my dad because it was a duty-free state and I wanted to buy some music equipment, and they put us up in the best hotel. We were not flush with cash at that time, but we were having the time of our lives hobnobbing with these millionaires, eating the best food that money could buy and drinking their champagne. Part of the convention was to have a night sailing on the Amazon, on some mega-luxurious hundred-foot yachts, each housing about twenty guests, with the same number of staff. My father and I were among the first fifteen guests to board one of the yachts. The other guests were mostly Americans, and we were all discussing how we could decide who had which room, when one woman suggested we put all the keys in a basket and each pick one out at random. It seemed a fair way of deciding and everyone agreed, and my dad pulled me to one side and said, 'Mike, get key number eight, it's my lucky number. Try to make it look like you are not looking, but pick out number eight.' My father was born on the eighth day of the eighth month, the Great Train Robbery was carried out on that date, and I was born in the eighth month, so that has always been his favourite number. I put my hand into the basket and picked out key number eight, without anyone realising that I was looking out of the corner of my eye at what I was doing. A few moments later the last five guests came on board, and one woman started complaining about the way the rooms had been allocated. But the others assured her it had been done fairly and properly, and that nobody knew what any of the rooms were like anyway. Besides, there were still five keys left in the basket and those might be the best rooms. However, without either of us realising, my dad had picked the presidential suite! It was magnificent. I asked him if he'd done it on purpose, and he assured me he hadn't, he had just wanted his favourite number eight. When the others saw our suite they couldn't believe it – good old lucky number eight!

That evening I fell sick with a fever, and my dad went out crocodile hunting with the Americans. The idea was not to kill the crocodiles, but just to tie them up, have your picture taken with them and then throw them back in the river. They all came back on board with a baby crocodile and stood on deck taking it in turns to have their picture taken with it. The woman who had moaned at us because we got the top suite was on deck, watching what was going on, and she was still making a fuss about the selection process for the cabins. After my dad held the crocodile and smiled for the camera, he nonchalantly handed the reptile to the loud woman and said, 'Here you go, your turn.' She freaked out completely and started screaming hysterically.

She was so loud that I could hear her screams from my cabin and they woke me up – but it was worth it when I found out what was going on.

Something else happened to me during that trip which I laugh about now, but which freaked me out a bit at the time. I was wandering in the red light district when I saw a magazine stand in the distance. One thing stood out a mile to me, the name Biggs on the front cover of one of the magazines. It said, 'Inside, see Ronnie Biggs.' I bought the magazine and there inside were photographs from a few years back of my father shagging some Brazilian model. I rushed back to show him, and he sat there smiling and just said, 'Yeah, I remember now, Armin must have taken those.' So now my father was a porn star too!

Although I had spent some time apart from my Ulla, we still had feelings for each other and she was still in my life, although perhaps not as seriously as the first two years, during which time I had been completely faithful to her. This time, I was seeing her and any other girl I fancied at the same time. We had some bad times, especially because Ulla was not reliable when it came to taking her contraceptive pill and on one occasion towards the end of our six years together she fell pregnant. I wanted her to have the baby, but she was adamant that she was too young and not ready for motherhood, and in the end she had the baby aborted, which hurt me and put a lot of strain on our relationship.

I needed something to throw myself into, and so I decided to build a rehearsal studio with my musician friends and band members, Pedro and Ivan, at the house which belonged to Ivan's mum. I had bought a lot of duty free equipment in the Amazon, but we needed more. My mother invited me to Switzerland and promised she could give me the money to buy some more duty-free equipment there, so I took her up on the offer. My spiritual father, Marcos, had gone there to make money from shell readings for our church in Rio, and he also stayed at my mum's house. My mother introduced him to several believers in the religion, and one of them turned out to be a Brazilian hooker who had settled in Geneva and who ran a brothel out of several apartments across the country. This hooker had a 23-year-old

Swiss boyfriend, and I became very friendly with him, and he offered me a job. It turned out that the 'madam' needed to change a lot of the apartments at which the prostitutes were based, as they were becoming known to the police, and he wanted me to help transfer all the equipment from one flat to another. That suited me, and the two of us began driving all over Switzerland with a van filled with circular beds, giant crosses, mirrors, whips, strap-on dildos and every sex aid imaginable. We had to transfer everything in the middle of the night, when nobody could see us, and I often thought how funny it would be if we got stopped by the Swiss police, and had to explain why all this equipment was in the back of the van. I spent most of my nights crashed out in various of these apartments, which were fine apart from the purple fluorescent lights! Not only had I landed on my feet with a well-paid job, but a new hooker came in from Brazil who had never been on the game in her life. The 'madam' told me that this woman, who was 32 and quite beautiful, wanted to have a shag before she went on the game, and I was happy to oblige. I had a nice relationship with her in between clients, and everything involved the use of condoms, so I felt quite relaxed about it. When it was time to go back to Brazil my mother had not raised the money, but my spiritual father stepped in and gave me it instead, and I bought all the gear I needed.

I did not want to risk being stopped at Customs in Rio, because I did not have the money to pay the duty on it, and feared I would have it confiscated, so I took all the equipment out of its boxes, laid it at the bottom of my case and covered it with all my dirty washing. On the flight home we were told there was a problem at Rio airport and we were landing at São Paulo instead. There was so much confusion when we landed that the Customs people just decided to let everyone go through without conducting any searches – magic! But before I could get through, there was an announcement saying we were being put on an international flight back to Rio. That meant clearing Customs again, so I ripped off all my international luggage labels and decided to tell them I was just coming from São Paulo. When I walked through Customs there was a kid in front of me with no bags, and when he told the officer he had come from São Paulo and therefore had no luggage he waved him through. I was up next and when he asked what was in my bags I told him I was a musician who had come from São Paulo and it was my equipment. He waved me through too, so I was home and dry.

We worked flat out to build the studio. The other guys had invested more money than I did, so my old man weighed in on my behalf by helping us to build it. He didn't have much to do with his life apart from receiving a few tourists, so he would be there every morning at 6.30 a.m. and work tirelessly with us until about 4 p.m. He put up the doors, the windows and really got everything ready for us. I was so proud of this 66-year-old, my father, who helped us build the studio with his bare hands. I was very tired from working all the time and began arguing a lot with Ulla. We realised that our love affair had run its course; our love-making had become mechanical and the spark was no longer there, so we parted once and for all, and a month later she left for Italy to continue her studies.

The studio opened and it was one of the best in town. In the first year we made lots of money and partied hard, but we were having too much fun to run the business properly and never used the money wisely. Rather than invest it to pay the next month's rent, we would go out and buy a kilo of dope so we had plenty to smoke – such was our irresponsible attitude. I had women coming out of my ears again, until I met up with a biology student called Juliet who knew how to put me in my place. She used to say I was too 'Biggs' for my boots, and would tell me I wasn't that good-looking or such a great musician. I needed someone like that to stand up to me, and I fell deeply in love with her, and for the first time in my life I was faithful to her all the time I was seeing her. She left me after about eight months, but we are still friends today.

At this time in Brazil there was a new craze of dance music called the Forro which took off in a big way. I became a big fan and started going to every party I could, especially as I was a good dancer and knew how to strut my stuff. It was also a great excuse to shag as many birds as possible, because these parties were one big pick-up opportunity. At one of these dance parties I met a girl named Bel and we started going out. I wasn't sure how much she liked me because she was always playing mind games, one minute saying we were an item and the next that we were not. I was confused and hurt, but I had fallen for her and went along with it, even though she was making a fool of me. She had a brother who was on the run from the police, and I even helped out by letting him hide out at my studio. We had been going out for about six months and I decided I was going to see her for the last time. I would take her out, and while I was having sex with her I planned to tell her it was over, just like that. We had our night out, got very drunk together and went back to her house where we started shagging through the night. At about 6 a.m. the phone rang, and her brother answered it. It was one of my best mates, Eric – with whom I shared a passion for football – and he asked if Bel was there. Her brother told him she was asleep and put the phone down on him. My friend rang back and before Bel's brother could hang up again he told him it was an emergency, and that there was a problem with my dad. He woke me up and handed me the phone, and Eric said, 'Mike, your dad has had a stroke man, I have taken him to the hospital, you had better come now.' I was shocked, because the night before my dad had been fine, but my immediate reaction was the awful fear that I was going to lose him.

Bel came with me to the hospital – the two of us still stinking of booze – and we found my father lying on a bed. As soon as he saw me he started crying. His speech was slightly slurred and he said, 'I can't remember my father's name, I can't remember my mother's name, I'm confused.' I told him not to worry, everything would be all right. I took him home and I wanted to care for him myself, so I paid for my work at the studio to be done for me and stayed at home with Rosa to look after my father. Something else happened to me at this time: I met a really beautiful girl named Manuela, who was really supportive to me while my dad was unwell. I think that made Bel jealous, and she felt she was losing me, because she then paid extra attention to me herself, and I was torn between the two. Manuela put off going on a trip to America to be with me, but she didn't like the fact that Bel kept calling me when I was with her. She asked me what I was going to do, but I did not know, and a week later she left for the United States. She is one of the few women I really regret letting go from my life, and had I not later met Veronica it would have remained one of the big regrets in my life.

I started drinking and smoking cigarettes heavily. There was also a problem when a neighbour we didn't get on with made Ivan's mother an offer to buy the house. We topped his offer, and a bidding war raged which pushed the price of the house up by $25,000, until we could go no higher and pulled out, which meant we would lose the studio. A few months later, just before the deal was due to be completed, the buyer pulled out, but by then we had lost our backers and could not step in. I was running out of money, and what little I had was going on medicine and speech therapy for my father. I had to start earning money somehow, so I approached one of the top Forro bands, called Forrocacana, and asked if I could become their roadie; they told me to go and do one gig for them and see how it worked out. I had been working on stages since I was six years old, and if there was one thing I knew in my life it was how to make it work and how a stage should be structured. I decided I was going to be the best roadie in town, so I polished every guitar and did a really professional job. They were impressed, and took me on full time. Having been used to life on the other side of the coin, I can't say it didn't hurt me a little bit to be working like this, but it was also a challenge, and it was the fastest way I could earn the money to ensure my father was properly looked after. There were people who looked down on me – they couldn't accept that the boy who was once the star and who mixed with some of the biggest names in rock was now carrying other people's instruments. But it made me realise who my true friends were, and I shall never forget – or forgive – the ones who gave me the cold shoulder.

We were doing a minimum of four gigs a week in different states, which meant lots of travelling. I mastered my job to a fine art, and within 25 minutes of arriving at a venue I would have the stage ready and the instruments tuned, which gave me plenty of time to go and have a beer and a joint and chat up a few women. Everyone in the band was amazed because I would have everything ready before they had finished their lunch. Some of the band members really respected me, but there were others who treated me like a prat, because I was the roadie. But I was having a good time and through all the touring I met sound engineers, lighting engineers and bouncers, and I know they will be there for me if I ever tour as a musician in Brazil. During one trip I met an American who was dealing acid, and I introduced him to some people I knew who were looking to buy. He did some business with them, but he also knew the authorities were after him and he wanted to flee back to America. He did not want to get caught with his acid so he gave me a parting gift – 10,000 sheets of acid. I did not want to become a dealer so I started handing it out free of charge, which made me very popular. I had remained popular with the women too, even though many of them still knew me as Michael from The Magic Balloon Gang.

My dad's condition improved enough for him to start receiving tourists again, so we were both bringing in a bit of money and our quality of life improved. I started seeing a new girl, Joanna, who fell deeply in love with me, and my dad really liked her. One time I went away for four days with the band, and on the last night I was desperate to get home. Our band was always last on-stage, because they were the biggest, and that usually meant hanging around till about 2 a.m. before they went on-stage. On this occasion I hadn't had a shower for a couple of days, so I was filthy and didn't smell too fresh. The concert ended and I was rushing around clearing everything away so that I could get home and sleep and then see my father. As I was putting the last few instruments away I spotted two good-looking girls with fit bodies still hanging around, having a can of beer. I half recognised one of them and knew that they lived close to my neighbourhood, as this particular concert wasn't too far from my home. I looked and smelled terrible and the only thing on my mind was getting home as quickly as I could, so I went up to them and asked if they would give me a lift home. They were a bit wary at first, but when I told them that I didn't live too far away they agreed to drop me off. There was still one musician hanging around, who was drunk by now, and he asked me what I was doing. I told him the two girls were going to give both him and me a ride home, and I also threw in the fact that I'd heard the brunette say she fancied him, although I invented that just to make him hurry up.

The girl with the lighter hair was very sexy, with her short skirt and lovely long tanned legs, and she started being a bit cocky towards us, saying, 'Come on, "stars", hurry up.' That annoyed me a bit because I felt she was overdoing it. Plus, I was very grubby and didn't feel particularly attractive, especially standing next to this sexy girl. We got in their car and as we approached my house I said, 'Hey, why not come in and we'll have a joint for the road?' They liked the idea and the four of us went in and sat on my settee having a drink and smoking a joint. I started speaking to the cocky one and asked her name, and she told me it was Veronica. The other two fell asleep as by now it was 5 a.m. and Veronica and I started kissing passionately. I thought I was going to be able to take her to my room, but she said she had to go, and she woke her friend and they left. We were due to go on the road again that same afternoon, so I asked if I could have her number and call her when I got back.

I was still going out with Joanna, and my dad felt she was someone I should hang on to, but when I returned from that next run of gigs I telephoned Veronica. I carried a beeper at the time and Joanna was sending me regular messages because she liked me so much, and I knew I was going to break her heart. But I liked the fact that Veronica was very direct and open minded, and knew exactly what she wanted, and I wanted her. I tried to be romantic with her at first, but I could read in her eyes that she was saying, 'Cut the crap, take me home and fuck the daylights out of me. I don't want any of this romantic crap, I have come on to you because I want to shag you.' Here was a woman after my own heart, she thought like a man – like me in fact, and I liked that. Nor did Veronica care about my reputation, which helped, and we started seeing each other on a regular basis. It was coming up towards the end of the year and the band were due to perform a concert at a paradise beach resort, so I invited Veronica to come with me. She was a bit reluctant because she didn't know any of the other girlfriends, and they were very mean because they would say things in front of her like, 'Mike swaps his girlfriend every weekend, so this one won't last long.' But she came along anyway.

While we were away I started having some problems with the band's manager, and we argued over how much money I was owed. Veronica was very supportive, and she kept pulling me aside and telling me to calm down, and she gave me some good advice, telling me to stand my ground and that she backed me, even offering to loan me the money I needed to tide me over. I was quite taken aback, because this wasn't her fight, and I really respected her for arguing my corner. The arguments soured my working relationship with the band and when I went home and discussed it with my father, he agreed that I should quit. He was earning money again and he told me I should go back to being a musician, and that he would support me as best he could. That was great news for me, and so I hung up my roadie boots and went back to pursuing a career as a musician. But even though my dad and I agreed on so many points, because I was living back at home full time, which caused a bit of a problem for me, I started clashing with my dad over silly things, such as what time I was getting home. He started criticising my lifestyle and we argued quite badly. I was 24 and had never had these problems before; I didn't need him telling me what to do and I realised I couldn't carry on living under his roof any more. By coincidence, Veronica was also having some problems at home, and was considering moving to the north of Brazil to live with a friend. I saw an opportunity and spoke to her about the situation. I told her it would be wrong to give up on her studies, and suggested she moved into a little apartment I had found, and she agreed. I then told my father I was moving out, but said I would need to take my laundry to the house if he didn't mind, and also eat there once in a while. He didn't want to lose me, and in any case it was my house, so he was happy for me to use it as I pleased. He also offered me a job. He was hosting a weekly barbecue for tourists and he knew I was a good barbecue cook, so he asked me to do the cooking at these weekly events. Money was tight for me, and I was happy to take the job. It was a hard life for me at the time as I was cycling around town on a pushbike, renting out my PA equipment, trying to get odd jobs and rehearsing whenever I could and getting my band together. I also invested what money I had in building a studio in a cultural centre in Rio called the Progress Foundation; but it switched presidents and the new president screwed me to the tune of $10,000, because he wouldn't let me carry on building my studio there, which meant all my time, effort and money went to waste. I bounced back when I heard that a friend of mine named Carlos was opening his own studio. I went to see him and showed him some of my songs, and as we were talking he told me he had not got any clients yet. I offered to get some for him, because I had a contacts book with three hundred musicians in it, and in return he offered to produce my album for me, so we came up with a good arrangement for us both. I also contacted another friend who is an accordionist, pianist and arranger called Chico Chagas; he worked for free on all my recordings, and always believed in my musical potential, along with my friends Pedro Barreto, Eric and Ivan.

Things picked up further when I received an invitation to play percussion at the Montreux Jazz Festival for Roberta Do Recife, who was the daughter of renowned Brazilian musician Robertinho Do Recife. I was going to be paid to perform, but I was told I would have to pay the airfare myself. My mother worked for Swissair, so I believed she could get me a cheap ticket, and the wages would just about cover the cost of the trip. I knew it would be cool to play at the festival, and whenever I bumped into someone who had looked down on me for being a roadie, I couldn't help but let slip that at my next gig I'd be on the same bill as Al Jarreau, Herbie Hancock and many other of the world's top jazz musicians. At the last minute my mother failed to come up with the ticket, but my dad stepped in and handed me $800 to buy one instead. I hadn't been living with him, and we weren't at that time on the best of terms, so this was a fantastic gesture on his part – it touched me a lot. My father and I needed our own space to live our own separate lives, but it still hurt me to live apart from him, and Veronica, as a student of psychology, could see that it was affecting me.

However, a suitable distraction presented itself when Veronica announced that she thought she might be pregnant. She had it confirmed, and I didn't know what to do for the best, but I said I would support whatever decision she made. Veronica spoke to her family about it and then told me she wanted to have the baby. I suggested to her that we should both move out of the bedsit and back into my house until we made enough money to move out again. I told my father about the baby and said I was going to need my room again, but he was very happy to have his son back in the house. In fact, he and Veronica started having a beautiful relationship. I would arrive home and the two of them would be sitting there having a glass of wine and chilling out together, having maybe been to the cinema together or out for a meal. My father was allowed a glass of wine a day, but was drinking more like two and a half glasses, but I turned a blind eye to his one pleasure. I had been responsible for him giving up his joints, after we went to the doctor and I let it slip that he was still smoking dope. The doctor said it wasn't a good idea for a 69-year-old man who'd suffered a stroke, so dad gave it up, but not before berating me for 'grassing' him up.

With my father's seventieth birthday looming he decided to throw his last big party. He wanted it to be his last big bash before he retired to a quieter life – Ronnie Biggs's farewell to the limelight. A mate of his had invited him to live on a farm outside Rio and help him breed carp, and the old man was seriously considering it. The Jazz Festival was in June and July and the old man's party was going to be in August, and I promised to be back in time to organise everything for it. Veronica wanted to come to Montreux with me, and when she told her grandfather he gave her the money for her ticket and told her to go and have a honeymoon with me, even though we weren't married. Roberta knew Veronica and kindly made arrangements for us to have a luxurious double bedroom in the hotel overlooking the lake, and we had a fantastic couple of weeks.

We went from Montreux on to Geneva to stay with my mother. She had not yet met Veronica and, like all mums, she wanted to check her out. Both women have strong personalities and they clashed without needing to use words, although they never actually had an argument. We lasted a week there and then had to get out. We had open air tickets and were not ready to go back to Brazil, so we decided to fly to London and spend a few days there, staying with Nick Reynolds, walking all around London and having a great time sightseeing. Veronica's birthday was coming up, so I ran into town before we left Switzerland and bought a Swiss Army watch I knew she had her eye on. Before we had left Brazil, Veronica's family wanted to buy her a car for her birthday, and when we went to the showroom there was a choice between a modest runaround or an imported top-of-the-range sporty number. Money was not an issue for her family, but when I said to Veronica's grandfather that I didn't fancy the idea of my pregnant girlfriend driving around Rio in a car that would draw unnecessary attention to her, he turned to me with a smile of agreement, and I think that won over her family because they realised how much I cared about her and that I wasn't just a money-grabber.

When we arrived back in Rio after our European adventure, Veronica's mother and grandmother were waiting for us. As Veronica hugged her grandmother, her mother hugged me and whispered in my ear, 'Mike, Veronica's grandfather has died. What am I going to tell her?' I was in a state of shock, and Veronica turned around and asked, 'Where's Granddad?' She knew he would normally have been there to meet her too, because she had a very special relationship with her grandparents, and she just said, 'He's dead, isn't he?' Her mother nodded sadly and Veronica lost it, crying and screaming. I tried to comfort her, but she was naturally devastated, and upset because he would not get to see his great-grandchild. We left the airport, and I suggested that they drop me at my house and then let Veronica go back with them to spend time with her family. I had a happy and relaxed reunion with my father, and told him Veronica's sad news. The next day we started preparing for Dad's seventieth birthday party.

8. DAYS OF FREEDOM

Ronnie Biggs liked to party, and because he had previously celebrated both his twenty years of liberty in Rio, and also his sixtieth birthday, he was naturally expected by everyone to throw a big bash to mark his seventieth birthday in August 1999 – and he was not about to disappoint anyone. The plan was to throw a party at our home in Rio de Janeiro for more than a hundred guests from abroad and a further hundred from Brazil; the guest list included some of the crime world's most legendary figures. These included one of my father's oldest friends, Bruce Reynolds, the man who had masterminded the Great Train Robbery some 45 years earlier – either one of the most audacious crimes in British history, or one of the worst, depending on which side of the fence you sit. Also there were Dave Courtney, well known in the UK, plus Roy Shaw whose book has also been a hit there. From the media world, we had Gus Dudgeon, the music producer who worked with Elton John on *Goodbye Yellow Brick Road*, and Tony Hoare, one of the writers from the *Minder* television series, so it was quite a crew who gathered. However, my father had already had his first stroke more than a year before then – in February 1998 – and he was a bit worried because he was not in the best of health and didn't want the stress to add too much to his problems. It was therefore down to me to organise things. We never had any PR people to organise things, so news of the party spread simply by word of mouth. We also knew that the newspapers loved Ronnie Biggs and were always happy to report on his latest activity; whenever there was nothing to write about, especially in the late 1970s and early 80s, they would produce a story on Ronnie Biggs. I had just had a fantastic time in Switzerland, playing at the Montreaux Festival, and then spent a couple of weeks in London with Veronica. So I was keen and excited on my return to Brazil to get to work, organising the party. It was lucky that I'd had the holiday, in order to deal with the efforts I was going to have to make, as well as looking after Veronica following the death of her grandfather. With the numbers coming to the party, I was rushing around buying more than a thousand cans of beer, several crates of champagne, fifty kilos of meat and masses of soft drinks, as well as organising all the chairs and tables. I also had to arrange for a barman, so I contacted a Scottish friend of ours who ran a Scottish pub in Rio. He was quite a character, who had moved from Scotland with his wife to open this pub in Rio, and it had been going very nicely until suddenly a gay bar opened across the road. A second gay bar soon followed and within three to five months, there were eight gay bars in the same street and it became the gay capital of Rio. Our macho Scottish friend would not have gays in his pub, but that meant his flow of customers rapidly diminished, because the straight men did not want to be seen drinking in the area. So I had to laugh when one day he called me up and said, 'Michael, fuck it, I have painted my bar pink! If you can't beat 'em, join 'em.' Believe it or not, his bar is the only one left in the street, because the other pubs closed and the gay capital moved elsewhere. Our Scottish friend's establishment is now a lesbian bar, and is doing great business.

Ronnie's birthday party was a great success, with lots of media interest, and I think the old man felt that as it was going to be his last big party, his last big celebration, he really wanted to make it a great night. Unfortunately, he was proved right. My dad was seventy on 8 August 1999 and he really wanted to go for it, but it took quite a lot out of him because it went on right through the night. In fact the partying went on all week. We were expecting the police to gatecrash the party at some point, because that was something they had done ten years earlier at my father's sixtieth party. On that occasion, the neighbours had complained about the noise being made by a rock and roll band we had in the back garden, but when the police arrived they ended up joining the party! When they left, they were hugging my dad in a drunken state and telling him it was one of the best parties they'd ever been to. The police did not come to this party, however, maybe because there was no rock band to annoy the neighbours. My old man was not allowed to drink too much, so he took the opportunity to berate his friends in some good-natured banter because they were drinking all his beer while he was having a glass of wine – although I knew he was having a sneaky beer when he felt like it too. My father was very tired during this week of partying, and Gus Dudgeon, Breiti from *Die Thoten Hosen*, and Nick Reynolds pulled me to one side and said I must tell my father to stop, otherwise he would not last much longer. I could see he was right, but I couldn't confront my father during his party, not with all those guests there, because he would have just told me to fuck off. But once the party was over, he knew he would have to take things easy. It was going to be his last party, then he was going to retire.

To coincide with reaching seventy, Dad was going to do an advert for the Advance Hair Studios, a company which replaces lost hair. This was the company which used celebrities, such as former England cricket captain Graham Gooch, to promote its products. The ad had been fixed up by a dear friend of the family at the time, Bob Starkey, an Australian former guitarist for the Skyhawks and a man who was making a film about the life of Ronnie Biggs, although later he was to fall out with me in a big way. Starkey brought the owner of Advance Hair Studios to Brazil and they set about working on the advert. It was around this time I noticed that my father was really becoming tired, and did not bounce about with his usual energy. It was now about eighteen months since he had suffered his first stroke, but he was a strong man and appeared to have made virtually a full recovery. But I could see the stress in his face, and I kept urging him to take it easy. When Dad had suffered his first stroke I was halfway through recording an album, but I had to quit that to take care of him. After the party, my life started taking shape again and when I received a telephone call from the studio owner asking me to go back and finish the album, I jumped at the chance. I had finished four tracks and on 22 September 1999 a month after the party, the telephone rang as I arrived at the studio and it was for me. On the other end of the line was Veronica. She simply said, 'Your father has had another stroke, come back home.'

I rushed back to the house and I found my dad. He did not look well and he was still speaking, but with a croaky voice, and his speech was slurred. I told him, 'Dad, do not try to speak, because it will do some damage.' But he said, 'Why? I can speak, you can understand me.' But he was mumbling, and I said, 'No I can't, stop, let me take you to the hospital.' My father did not qualify for treatment on the Brazilian National Health Service as he had no social security number. (He was in Brazil under a deportation order which prevented him from marrying or working, but he no longer had to sign in with the federal police anymore, thanks to the help of a lawyer, Wellington Mousinho, in November 1987.) As he didn't qualify for medical help at that time, I took him to the Fourth Centenary, a private hospital in Rio. After we arrived his condition deteriorated. They put a tube in his nose to feed him and they put nappies on him, and I became really frightened. I moved very close to him and I said, 'Dad, can you hear me? If you can hear me give me an OK sign.' Although his eyes were closed, he gave me the thumbs up, so I knew he could hear me and understand me. I was relieved, and I just sat there and cried. I could remember after the first stroke that he couldn't really remember dates of birth, the names of his parents, or things like that, so I decided to test his memory. He couldn't open his eyes so I said, 'Dad, I need to know everything is working inside your head, so I am going to ask you some questions. Am I your oldest son?' He gave me the thumbs down, meaning no, and I said, 'Nice,' because he knew what he was doing. I then said, 'Dad, am I your middle son?' Again he put his thumb down, so I said, 'Okay, your mind is working. Beautiful! Now, Dad, I am going to need some money to pay for this hospital. I think I know where the money is. Is it inside the lampshade?' He again gave me the thumbs up, and I knew his brain was working OK. He still couldn't open his eyes, and it was a very tense moment for me. I didn't know how long it was going to take for my father to recover. I assumed it would be like the first stroke, and within six months my dad would be speaking normally again and we'd just resume our lives, but as it turned out that was not going to happen.

My father looked very frail lying there in bed, and I was concerned about how I would keep things going. Fortunately we had some money coming in. Just recently Dad had been negotiating with a computer games company. They wanted to develop a Great Train Robbery game, which was to be their first non-violent computer game, and they signed up Ronnie Biggs. Before his stroke, my father had already decided he was going to split the profits with Bruce Reynolds, so although I needed the money I couldn't go back on my dad's word, as he'd promised Bruce 50 per cent of this deal. I had to get my dad out of hospital because after three and a half weeks the bills were mounting up fast, but at least the doctors had told me he was well enough to go home and try and recover there. But I needed to bring in a nursing team which could look after him 24 hours a day – he could not dress himself, he could not shave, he could not feed himself; all he could do was sit in bed and watch television. The home-care team cost the equivalent of about £40 a day, which in Brazil is a lot of money, and it mounted up fast. My income had stopped because I had stopped work on the album for a second time to help look after Dad. Furthermore, while he was laid up in bed, Dad was unable to greet tourists, which had been his main source of income for some time. So I flew to England to finalise the deal for the computer game and sort out the payment, which gave us enough money to survive for about a year. I was also visiting England to chase up some $5,000 which was still owed to us from the advert with Advance Hair Studios. Dad said it appeared we had been screwed on the deal by Bob Starkey, but his attitude was that we had at least still made $15,000, which was better than nothing. When I returned home, I could see the old man had become very depressed. He told me he didn't need the home-care team any more either, because they had been with us for a couple of months and were costing too much money. He said he could manage if Veronica and I gave him the drugs instead; if we all worked as a team then we wouldn't need any outside help. He appeared to be doing fine, but it wasn't always easy to keep track of him because he woke up very early and would wander around the house, still doped up, doing his own thing. I saw this as a sign of recovery, although I still felt he was depressed within himself.

One morning I woke up and went into his room to give him his drugs, but he was not there. I was singing and whistling, walking through the house looking for him, as I assumed he was up and about doing his own thing. I couldn't find him in the lounge or the kitchen so I checked the garden, as he often went out there to check on his plants, but he wasn't there either. I wandered back into the house and walked up to his bathroom; I shall never forget the sight that greeted me as I opened the door. There was blood on the walls; there was blood on the ceiling. I looked at the floor and there was blood everywhere. My Dad was lying face down, with a knife by his side; he had cut his wrists and he was bleeding to death. Time stood still as my mind flashed to my wife, who was by now eight months pregnant. Then I snapped out of it, rushed and grabbed a couple of towels and tied them around his wrists to stop the blood pouring out. My father was continually passing out and then coming to, and I could see that he was trying to say that he was sorry, and that he couldn't go on any more. By this time Veronica had joined me and right there and then she started having contractions. It was six-thirty in the morning and I was by myself, so I had to take charge very quickly. After tying up Dad's wrists I carried him back to bed, with blood dripping all over the place. Rosa, our housekeeper, arrived and when she saw what was going on she went completely frantic. I tried to calm everyone down, Veronica was still having contractions, the old man was losing blood fast, and the maid was crying and screaming hysterically. I had to keep my head together. I rang a doctor friend of mine and blurted down the phone, 'For the love of Christ come quickly because my dad is dying.' The doctor came immediately; he cleaned up the wounds and left the wrists tied, and he called another doctor to sew up the cuts. Luckily, he had cut the main vein only on the left arm; the right arm wasn't that bad. The left one was serious, and had I woken up twenty minutes later my father would have been dead. Meanwhile Veronica had stopped her contractions by doing some deep, slow breathing, and by talking to our unborn child, explaining to it that it wasn't yet the right time to be born, that things would have to wait for a few more days yet.

We were all in a very bad position. My father was still very depressed; my wife had also gone downhill and feared she would lose the baby. On top of that, I could not leave my dad alone again, which meant bringing in people to care for him once more. I couldn't work, look after the house, pay the bills *and* look after my dad – I was only 25 after all. Another problem presented itself, because my dad was looking for ways in which to vent his pent-up anger and frustration, and unfortunately he turned on Veronica, who was heavily pregnant but still waking up at 3 o'clock every morning to give him drugs. He needed someone to hate, and he ended up hating Veronica over nothing. But I couldn't, blame Dad because I knew he wasn't thinking properly; it was the effects of the stroke, the drugs, and the depression which had led to his suicide attempt. One minute Dad would be telling Veronica how much he hated her, and that she had taken over his house and he didn't want her there; then ten minutes later the realisation of what he'd said would hit him and he would burst into tears, crying, 'What am I saying to this girl? I love her, she is a daughter to me.' My father was so confused at times that he would swear the day was Friday when it was Monday, and he was ready to fight with anyone and everyone in the house to argue his case. I think that inside he was frightened by the fact he was no longer in total control of his mind, and he would fight to be right because every victory was a major triumph for him. I could not get too angry with my dad because he didn't know what he was saying, and I was just trying to keep the family together, so no grudges were ever held because I knew at that stage his mind was going.

I had to think of ways to keep some money coming in, so I bought a computer to give me access to the Internet. My idea was to set up a Ronnie Biggs website, because the Internet boom was beginning and I figured I could make a lot of money from advertising space on a site, because there was still a lot of interest in my dad all over the world. After an initial bit of bother over the registration of the domain names, Ronnie Biggs.com and Ronnie Biggs.co.uk, when I discovered that they had been registered by someone else, we set up the website and had it all ready to go, when Veronica woke me up to tell me she was going to have our baby. We were lying in bed one morning when she suddenly nudged me and said, 'Mike, it's time, my waters have broken.' We left the house at about 6 a.m. on 22 January and went to the hospital. Veronica had to give birth by Caesarean section. As she was lying there being cut open, I filmed everything with my video camera, and I suddenly started remembering the moment I found my dad on the bathroom floor. As they were cutting through the layers of muscle and fat my knees nearly went, but I told myself to act like the strong husband and father, and the next thing I knew, at 8.52 a.m., weighing in at 3.33kg and standing – almost – at 46 cm, Ingrid was born. I was as shocked as every new parent – we had a new face in the house and it looked like me! The doctor said we had a tough one there, because she was screaming and fighting, and I looked at her and could see myself. I knew this would breathe new life into my dad when he saw his tiny granddaughter, so I went and picked him up and took him back to the hospital. It was a wonderful family moment with Dad crying and getting really emotional.

It wasn't long before the *News of the World* got in touch because they wanted to take some pictures of Ronnie with Ingrid, the proud grandfather posing with the newborn baby. I knew that I couldn't present my dad in the mental and physical state he was in at that time, especially with his wrists the way they were, but we needed the money, so I told the newspaper to wait until my father had got himself together. I now had 24-hour home care to help my old man eat, drink, bathe and take his drugs, plus I had an extra mouth to feed, so it was killing me financially. Somehow I had to provide, and it was time to step up the website idea because I felt that might be the answer.

But first of all there was one more problem to sort out. At the time that Dad had his second stroke, I owned two rehearsal studios in a house in Rio, and next door to the house was a fitness centre. They would start their fitness sessions at 6 a.m. and their music was very loud, particularly as we had not long gone to bed after being up all night recording. It was against the law in Brazil to make noise before 7 a.m., so we had a few chats with them and complained about the noise. In return, the owner of the fitness centre complained about the smell of marijuana wafting from the studios into his garden, so a battle between the two of us went on for several weeks. The centre had a swimming pool in the garden, so we were throwing dog mess into the pool and whatever else we could find. The problem was only resolved because the owner of the house with the rehearsal studios had to sell up; we were forced to move out and I put all my equipment into storage. That was when I started working full time on the Internet to try and survive. With the website and our great business plan all ready, we were just about to seal a £100,000 deal with some investors when the Dot Com bubble burst. I was screwed, but I opened the site anyway and I was getting at least 1,500 people hitting it every week. It was a great shame because I had the perfect brand for all the investors, but all the money dried up. One of my partners at the time was a rich kid whose father had moved to Miami and left him with an apartment right on Ipanema Beach, the most expensive square mile in

South America. The boy didn't even live there because he had another apartment he shared with his mother a couple of blocks away, so the one on the beach became our office. There were six of us building the website, and although we were hard up we were overlooking the ocean, smoking dope, working day and night, and having a good time!

The only money Ronnie had been able to make for some years had been from tourists who visited the house to see the old man and enjoy what we dubbed the Biggs Experience. At the beginning of 2000, hundreds of Manchester United supporters were arriving in Brazil because Sir Alex Ferguson's team were playing at the Maracana stadium in the World Club Championship. My father said he wanted to start greeting people again and bring some money in from the Biggs Experience. He said, 'I want to start being myself again, I don't want to be an invalid.' He was adamant, so I said, 'Let's go for it.' We printed more T-shirts, which he signed, because we knew these United fans were going to phone in and look for us. People came a dozen at a time to meet the famous train robber, have their photograph taken with him and sit, fascinated by the stories he had to tell. My father still had to spend a lot of time in bed, so I used to greet the people and then he would come out, shake their hands and have his picture taken with them. It was a bit of a sad scene, because I would welcome the tourists, tell them some stories, put on some videos and then Ronnie Biggs came out at the end to shake their hands, have some photos taken and hand out the T-shirts. It was depressing but it was putting food on our table and we were working as a team again, and at least it kept the visitors happy. When the extra visitors were in town, Veronica came up with the idea to cash in as much as possible. Up until then we charged only $10 for the Biggs Experience, for which you got a T-shirt, some good stories and a photograph of you shaking hands with the man himself. The T-shirt read, 'I know someone who went to Brazil and met Ronnie Biggs – honest!' Dad's philosophy was to keep the price cheap and then people might buy two or three T-shirts rather than just the one, but Veronica persuaded him to double the price, because she was convinced we were undercharging. Dad agreed, but wrote down, 'You pair of mercenaries!' It was weird because I could see that my dad was really fighting hard, whereas other times it looked as if he had given up. The money we were making meant I could afford to pay for my father to watch television, which was his last real pleasure in life as he couldn't speak, and only read or write a small amount. Our little income meant I could pay for the 120 channels and I could also pay our maid Rosa, who had been with us for twenty years and who had lent us her life savings so I could pay for the home-care team for my father after his second stroke.

However, things were getting tougher with every passing week and there was no way out for me, we were just getting deeper and deeper in debt. A small respite came when the owner of a small but established music studio rang to tell me his partner had left him, and taken all his equipment. He knew mine was in storage and asked me to put it in his studio, with us then splitting the profits. So my days consisted of greeting tourists in the morning, working on the website during the day and then rehearsing in the studio at night with a small band I had put together – and I had a young daughter to worry about now as well, so I was under quite a bit of pressure. I spotted an opportunity because the owner of the studio was a bit of a hippy, so I offered to buy him out and he accepted. It meant I had one more debt to contend with, but I knew the studio would generate enough money to pay that off in a matter of months. However, there were more complications ahead as I had to leave Ipanema Beach and work from home, because I couldn't afford to pay the website workers or also the maintenance charges on the apartment, which still had to be paid even though it was rent-free. To keep costs down as much as I could, I was cycling between the three venues – my home in Santa Teresa, the beach apartment and the studios – but when I got home at night, drenched in sweat, my father would moan because there was no food on the table and Veronica would tell me that our phone was going to be cut off because we hadn't paid the bill. I had no money so I began to borrow some. I went to my dad's friends, some of whom were very wealthy people, asking for money for my dad's medication and home help. They had known my dad for thirty years and handing out £20,000 would probably have made no difference to their lives, but they all said no and turned their back on him. Out of a hundred friends who came to Brazil to help celebrate his seventieth birthday, there were probably only about six who put some money up. I then turned to Veronica's family for help and her grandmother agreed to lend me some money. But my life was frantic and I started losing it; after paying the bills I was drinking beer like an animal and smoking dope and cigarettes. The next thing I knew, I was looking at £30,000 worth of debt. I owed friends, family, business associates, banks, credit-card companies, even the maid. I had one bit of help when a Scottish friend by the name of Brian Running invested $10,000 in my website, as a goodwill gesture just to tide me over. Brian had been the chief photographer on a cruise ship and had become friends with my father over the years when his ship had docked in Rio. My father and Brian had enjoyed many long drinking sessions together in the Plaza Maua, which was the red-light district of the docks area. It was Brian who had paid for the thousand cans of beer at my father's seventieth birthday, although he made me promise not to tell my father – a promise I kept only until Brian had left the country. When I did tell my dad he burst out laughing! Brian was also kind enough to fly me to England for a month at that time to look for more potential backers, but no business that I spoke to seemed to want their name associated with the name Ronnie Biggs.

The old man became increasingly depressed. He could see how much trouble I was in and he could see how his fit, good-looking, happy, young musician son was losing hair and gaining weight; I was suddenly becoming a balding, chubby, psychological wreck and my Dad knew it was all down to his illness. While I was in England, I tried to launch an amnesty campaign for my father, and a company even designed a logo for me. The company wanted to use Ronnie Biggs in an advertising campaign. The idea of the advert was to show my father on a train, but when the police boarded the train to capture him he had disappeared, and all that was left was a laptop displaying the catchphrase of the product, 'So cheap it's criminal.' It was a clever idea, but unfortunately the Advertising Standards Council banned it. While in England I also met up with Nick Reynolds, and he put me in touch with a music company called Almafame, which is owned by a long-time friend of Nick and Bruce by the name of Kevin Crace, and his partner Mark Norden. I told Kevin about my idea of an amnesty campaign, and he fixed up a meeting for me with some contacts of his at the *Sun* newspaper. The *Sun* were not interested in the amnesty campaign, but they told me that if my father wanted to come back to Britain, then we could talk business, and they would take care of all the costs involved, including bringing him home and securing all the necessary documents. I told them I wasn't interested in their idea, but they made me feel welcome and suggested I put the idea to my father. I returned to Brazil – my trip to England having been a failure – and did not want to tell him about the meeting with the *Sun*, but we were still behind the eight-ball. I said, 'Dad, there is a proposition on the table but I don't want to take it.' He couldn't speak properly because of the stroke and when I told him what it was, he wrote down, 'I do.' This all happened soon after I stepped off a ten-hour flight and I knew I would not be able to live the rest of my life in the knowledge that I had taken my father back to captivity in England, so I told him to forget it. I went and put Ingrid to bed and Dad came into the bedroom and he wrote on his pad, 'I want to go.' I told him NO, but for one week he would not communicate with me except to say, 'I want to go. I want to fight.'

At this time, we had been invited to go to a farm for a weekend break by Veronica's family, but I couldn't afford to take my dad. Then a tourist at the house, who we knew as 'Spider', heard us arguing and asked what the problem was. When I told him I needed £250 to go on this little holiday he went to his hotel and brought me the money. I couldn't believe it because I didn't know this guy from Adam, but he said, 'Your father has been a bit of a hero of mine all my life, I can afford the money, please let me pay for the trip and you can give me back the money whenever you have it.' That was a really nice gesture and it showed what my dad meant to some people who had followed his life story. If it hadn't been for Spider, we could never have taken that trip. We went to the farm and went on lots of walks with my dad in the woods, and all we could talk about was whether or not he should go back to England, and I was putting forward all the points against him returning. One of the friends who had been working on the Internet site, Gio, had been showing my dad the English newspaper headlines on the net, and they had seen the sentences being handed out to paedophiles. My dad turned to me and wrote, 'If we were in England and somebody molested Ingrid, they would get away with five years, whereas I have been ordered to serve thirty. I could be dead in six weeks, let me go back and fight, I want to go down fighting.' He had me by the balls. I could understand why this proud man wanted to go back and challenge the authorities, but it also meant I would be sending my old man to jail. How would they treat him once he was there, and how would I live with that decision for the rest of my life? Veronica was also against him going back; she even suggested selling the house if it meant finding the answer to our financial troubles.

Meanwhile, the *Sun* felt they might be on to a story, and they sent a small team of reporters out to Brazil to try and persuade us to do a deal with them. They talked to us on and off for about three weeks and eventually we reached an agreement with them, whereby they would take Ronnie Biggs back to Britain. One initial idea was to smuggle my father back into the country and declare him at immigration. It was felt it would be too difficult to get him out of Brazil as Ronnie Biggs, so the idea was to borrow the passport which belonged to someone's mother, then fly out a make-up artist to disguise my father to look like this old woman. He'd then book a seat on a regular scheduled airline flight, posing as this woman, and hopefully go home unnoticed. But after talking this through, we realised this was a recipe for disaster, and also felt we would be taking enough risks without breaking any extra laws, so we instead agreed that the *Sun* would fly him home officially, on a private jet. The return was set for two weeks into the future, but those plans were scuppered within a few days thanks to a press leak, and all hell broke loose on Wednesday 2 May. Kevin got a call at 8 a.m. from Mike Sullivan at the *Sun*, saying that a freelance journalist was on to the story, and Ron had to leave now. I first got a call from Nick Reynolds telling me that somebody had leaked to the press that an attempt was being made to bring Ronnie Biggs back to Britain. The next call I received was from Kevin Crace in England, and he told me to get my father and hide because all hell was about to be let loose. By this time we had no home-care team; my dad was looked after by the maid and the family, but he was also visiting a very good day centre which helped people who had suffered strokes, called the Oscar Clarke Centre. It was a public centre but the service was top quality, giving him speech and body therapy. When the phone call came, my dad was at the day centre, so I dropped everything and rushed to pick him up. The *Sun* reporters were there again and they said it was now or never, we had to get this story moving. The newspaper had planned to print spoof front pages on its first two early editions, then break the news in the edition after that.

It would be only a matter of time before our house would be swarming with reporters, photographers and camera crews, so I had to take my dad to a safe house. It was very disturbing for Veronica, who did not know what was going on back in the UK, to return home with Ingrid and be confronted by photographers putting their cameras in her face. I was born into that kind of environment and had become used to it, but she was not; we agreed she should move into a hotel. Fortunately we had a mate who liked to call himself the American Ronnie Biggs. He had escaped from America in a similar way to my father fleeing from Britain and was now exiled in Rio too, with two Brazilian children. He was very rich and had a big, secluded house, and he was happy for my dad to stay there. The *Sun* reporters were with us too, including Mike Sullivan, John Kay and John Askill, because they were not letting us out of their sight. But we had the first of several arguments because they wanted to produce a video camera and start filming what was going on. There was nothing about that in the contract they had drawn up, so I told them to forget any ideas of using the camera or I would pull the plug on the deal, and after arguing among themselves they reluctantly agreed. I think they accepted they were journalists, not film-makers. Meanwhile, we put a message on our answer phone directing callers to Kevin in London, and after the *Sun* hit the streets he was woken by the first call at 4.15 a.m. because the world's press was now on to the story.

And that's how Ronnie Biggs came to be flying back to England that Monday morning in May 2001. After all those years abroad, the exile's days of freedom were over.

9. BACK IN THE UK

My father was taken from our jet in a convoy of thirteen vehicles, supervised by Scotland Yard's Special Escort Group, who normally transport Britain's most violent criminals. Ronnie Biggs was not out to hurt anybody – I felt disgusted at the way the police overreacted to my father's voluntary return to his homeland. I went back inside the empty plane and Nick Reynolds came and sat by my side and said, 'Mike, he wanted to do it, he wanted to come back. Don't feel guilty about it.' He was right of course, not that it made me feel any better. My thoughts soon turned to my own immigration status, because I needed to be sure that the British authorities were going to let me into their country. An immigration officer came into the plane to interview me, and he asked me how long I wanted to stay in Britain. I said I didn't know, I told him it all depended on how long my father was going to be in jail. I told him that I wanted to be there to give my father moral support and to fight for his release. At first he said that I had to give him some kind of idea of how long I wanted to remain in Britain, he wanted a definite departure date, but it was impossible to know. I knew that had I told him I wanted to stay for six months, he would have stamped my passport, but that after six months I would have been kicked out of Britain. I also knew that if I then tried to re-enter the country, I would have been refused admission. I couldn't run that risk, so I did not give him a date. He was not entirely satisfied, yet he assured me I would have no problems obtaining a visa. He simply said, 'Here is a temporary visa, and don't worry because everything will sort itself out.' How wrong he was. I was given temporary admission for one month, which also gave me permission to work, and that at least gave me some hope that I would be able to survive in London.

I was taken off the jet and into a room where they wanted to search our luggage. We had brought with us three suitcases in all, one containing my clothes, another containing my father's clothes and some photographs, plus a third one full of videos, newspaper cuttings and material for the website. I was also carrying one of my most prized possessions, my guitar. The people from the *Sun* had arranged accommodation for me at a hotel in Kensington, and they had a car waiting to take me there. I was very tired – I'd had about an hour's sleep on the flight from Brazil – so I slumped into the car with Kevin Crace, who had helped set up the newspaper deal. On the way to the hotel, Kevin's mobile telephone did not stop ringing, and he was under pressure from everybody wanting a piece of the return of Ronnie Biggs. I was more concerned, however, with what the police might be doing to my dad. I had wanted to go along with them, just to explain to them about all the drugs he needed to take. He was all alone in their hands. I had given him a bag with all the drugs and prescriptions – he had to have seven different types of drug at different times of the day – but I wondered just how well they would look after him. One of the phone calls Kevin took was from Johnny Pickston and Gio, who had now arrived in London, so he told them to meet us at the hotel. Johnny later told me that there had been some resentment from the people of Brazil over the fact my father had returned to Britain. They had said, 'You spent thirty years here and now you are leaving, aren't we good enough for you any more?' Johnny had done his best to make them feel better about it.

When I got to the hotel later that morning I met Steve, the husband of Jane Wearing, Dad's solicitor, and the first thing he said to me was that I ought to get a suit because I would be attending a press conference. The funny thing was I had never owned a suit before. I looked like a third-world Pedro in a first-world country. Although my one and only concern was my dad in jail, I was now high profile, and in England, and I had to take care of my image. I was completely lost, and all I kept thinking was, 'Where is my dad? How is he? What is he going to eat? Who is going to help him eat? Who is going to give him his medication?' I had no answers to any of these questions and I was very concerned. To make matters worse, Veronica was on the phone to me in tears, saying she could see on the news what had happened. She asked me how my dad was and when we would be back together again, but I did not have the answers for her. I walked around my hotel room in a bit of a daze; but it was then I realised why my dad had picked Gio to accompany me in London. When I was told I needed a suit, Gio took charge of matters. He knew exactly where we were and he knew there was a Marks & Spencer and a shoe shop just around the corner, and he took me straight there to get me kitted out. Once inside the shop, Gio asked me my waist size, chest size and collar size, but all I gave him in return was a blank look. I was used to medium sized herring shirts and T-shirts ranging from medium to extra large. People in Brazil know how to dress properly when they want to, but it had never bothered me if I wore ripped jeans. I probably went shopping for clothes once a year because 90 per cent of my T-shirts came from shows or rock concerts, so I would go out and buy thirty pairs of underpants in one go and then not worry again for ages. It was the same with jeans or tennis shoes. At least there was one lighter moment during our shopping spree: Gio managed to cheer me up by making me laugh at the story of his arrival in Britain, because he said, 'Don't ever ask me to travel anywhere again with Johnny Pickston!' He told me that when they arrived in London, they walked through Customs without a hitch – until Johnny pointed at Gio and asked a Customs official, 'Aren't you going to search him?' That was the only invitation the official needed, and he called back Gio and went through his luggage.

Johnny Pickston and Gio are two other colourful characters who have played an important part in my father's life, and also mine. To know the real Pickston you have to understand his sense of humour, and my dad gave me countless examples of this. When I was about three we were all at the Copacabana Palace hotel, which is where the old man often went to meet tourists. We were relaxing by the pool with a legendary rocker, Rick Wakeman, when Rick took off his boots. My dad thought he would have a laugh, so he took Rick's boots and put them on, but the others turned the tables on him by throwing him into the pool. When my dad came up for air, he saw everyone standing on the side laughing their heads off, and he made a point of berating Johnny for laughing so loudly. That was the cue for the others to pick up Pickston and throw him into the pool too. But when Johnny came to the surface, he casually took out a soaking wet cigarette from his pocket and asked, 'Anyone got a light?' The others fell about laughing. On another occasion, Johnny was at a posh dinner with my father at the Copacabana Palace and his bottom false teeth were playing him up. When nobody was looking, he took them out and dropped them into a nearby coffee pot – God knows why! At the end of the dinner a well-to-do woman picked up the pot to pour herself a coffee, and Johnny's dentures fell into her cup. My father didn't meet Gio – who was living and working in Brazil teaching English – until his seventieth birthday, when he came along to help serve the drinks at the party, but Gio was one of the few people who went out of his way to help us and comfort my father after his second stroke, and even though he is in his thirties he struck up a sincere friendship with my old man. He stayed with me when I came to London, and helped on the website, and I do not think I could have survived without his help and friendship. In Brazil, my father was called a *Malandro* which is a term for someone who is smart and knows their way around situations. Gio was my London *Malandro*.

Having sorted me out with the right-sized suit, shirt and shoes, and a tie to match, Gio took me back to the hotel. There, I received a telephone call telling me I was allowed to visit my dad in Belmarsh prison that afternoon – where he had been transferred to – and take him some clothes. We grabbed some things and dashed straight off there in the car provided for us by the *Sun*. Amazingly, we drove through the throng of 35 or so waiting media without them realising who I was, so they failed to get photos or footage of me arriving at the prison.

Belmarsh is a maximum security prison and my visit was to prove something of a rude awakening. The call which told me I was allowed to visit my father had come from the governor himself, but when I arrived at the main gates the guards knew nothing about it. After a few phone calls I was allowed to proceed and I moved on to a search point, carrying my father's suitcase. I didn't know the rules and regulations concerning what you could or could not take in with you. I was carrying £1,000 in cash in my pocket, because I had just arrived in England and did not know how much money I'd need. But you are allowed to take in only £7.50, to use for teas, coffees and snacks. I asked the duty officer if he was going to make me walk back across the yard to the enrolment centre, where there are lockers to deposit your personal belongings during visits, and risk being photographed by the horde of snappers who I had managed to avoid the first time around. I told him it wasn't as if I was going to give the money to my dad to spend while inside, and he could count it when I came out, and I think they decided it was less hassle just to let me in.

People who subsequently came with me to visit my father in Belmarsh would aptly describe it as a 'draining' experience. As you approach the main entrance the first thing you notice are the armed police patrolling the car parks. Then you hear the Alsatians barking on the other side of the huge walls. Young mothers approach the doors clutching the hands of their little girls in pink flowery dresses and hats, and it strikes you how sad it is that the only contact these young children have with their fathers is their two-hour visit in a room full of strangers. As you progress through the check-in procedure you have to take off your shoes, belt and watch, and they are scanned separately, just as if you were passing through airport security, as the guards check for hidden cameras or recording devices. You are searched both on your way in and out, including looking inside your mouth to ensure you are smuggling nothing in. Your hand is stamped at two separate checkpoints, with one of those invisible markings which show up only under an ultra-violet light – rather like when you leave a theme park at Disneyland and want to be able to re-enter later the same day, only this is no Disney experience. The only thing you are allowed to carry on your person is the £7.50 cash for refreshments. When you finally reach the communal visiting area, just look to the right hand corner and you see a white-haired old man, my father, waiting patiently for his visitors. Then once you sit opposite him he pulls out a chart with the letters A to Z on one side, and the numbers 1 to 9 on the reverse, and he spells out the words he wants to relate to you, as he cannot speak. Or maybe he will pull out his pad and pen, and write down what he is trying to say. All the prisoners wear a fluorescent yellow or red stripe over their body, the kind a cyclist might wear, to distinguish them from the visitors, otherwise they are dressed casually in their own clothes. You look around the room and wonder what crime all these other men have committed, as they sit chatting to their family and friends. Sometimes small arguments break out, and as one visitor put it, the whole experience beats an episode of *EastEnders*!

So on my first visit to see my dad, I went on to the hospital wing. I have been to prisons in South America, but this was like everything you have seen in a bad movie. As far as I am concerned, when you have sick people in the health-care centre it should be clean, but this was quite dirty. I felt sure that if there was a sanitation inspection in Belmarsh, they would have closed that wing. For two months, there was a disposable rubber glove on one of the staircases. It was frightening because this was supposed to be among the best medical centres in the country. There were locked gates and intercom systems all along the corridors, and I couldn't believe it was necessary for my father to be in such a tight security prison. As if to 'welcome' him home, he even became Prisoner 002731 again – his old number from Wandsworth Prison. I assumed he would be moved from Belmarsh quite quickly, but I was wrong. I was also disappointed to learn that there were no televisions for the prisoners, because this was my father's one pleasure, since he couldn't read or write properly, and I found that a little cruel. When I finally reached the cell in which my dad was being kept, he was lying down and there were three nurses checking him out. It was a small cell with just a bed, a table, a toilet and a sink, both of which were made out of steel. I was introduced to a doctor who wanted me to help him translate all my father's drugs, because he needed to order more from the National Health Service and he wanted to check that the dosage matched that prescribed in Brazil. I looked at him as if he was mad, because he was the doctor, not me, but he looked lost. I had been giving my father these drugs for the past two years, but all I knew was that he had to have a certain dosage at certain times. After speaking with the doctor I was allowed to sit at the table and chat with my dad, but it was an awkward atmosphere because they kept three officers in the room with us. It was my father who typically broke the ice. It was the first time he had ever seen me in a suit, and he could hardly believe his eyes. We hugged each other and he wrote down, 'You look like a doctor from the clap clinic!' Only my father would have come up with something like that, and our tears of sorrow became tears of laughter. I could not understand why they needed three officers listening to our conversation. What a waste of time and manpower – it wasn't as if we were going to try and break out. We were in the medical wing of a top security prison, with cameras all over the place, and I felt I was entitled to some privacy with my father. This was just one of the excesses which always accompanied my dad's case. It was hard for me not to break down, but my dad wrote me a note which said, 'Do not break down in front of the slags, don't give them the satisfaction.' You do get a lot of nice prison officers, and I have met many beautiful people working in the prison, but you also get a few mean ones who quite enjoy seeing people suffer. They seem pleased to see people break down – I think they are a bit twisted. I was finding it hard to hold myself together but my dad wrote, 'Mike, don't cry in front of them, do this for me. I have been inside before, I know what it is like to be in prison, whereas you have never visited family in prison before so you had better start learning the rules now – do not break down in front of these pricks!' I was and am very proud of my father, I always knew he was a strong man, but I didn't realise just how strong until I saw him in Belmarsh. I had an hour with my father before I had to leave, and I left him in reasonably high spirits. I then asked when I could next visit him. However, because he was a Category A prisoner, I was told I could visit him only once every fifteen days. How could they do that? The guy was old and sick, what were they doing? But it was time to leave and the governor allowed our car into the prison grounds so we could leave without attracting too much attention from the media. As we drove away, I looked at the high walls and the tight security and I made myself feel better about the visit by saying that I felt sure this would be only a temporary home for my father until they moved him to an open prison or a hospital. I was cheered, too, by the sight of the crowd of people outside the main gates who were waving Union Jacks and banners saying, 'Welcome Home Ron', and it was nice to know we already had some support from many sympathisers.

I knew from this support that I had to launch a campaign to get my dad out of prison. In the middle of the night before we left Brazil I had returned to my house and found 8,000 e-mails waiting for me, as news of my father's return to the UK spread around the world. I'd just ripped the hard drive out of my computer and packed it with the rest of the things I was taking with me, knowing I would have to deal with it later. I did not have access to a computer when I first arrived in Britain for a few days, so one of the first things I asked Gio to find me was a laptop so I could carry on receiving e-mails. When I was finally able to log on via the laptop, I had another 3,000 e-mails waiting for me. It was our policy to reply personally to each and every e-mail we received. When we were all living happily in Rio my father would provide the replies, but now it was up to me. There were e-mails from supporters, opponents, nutcases, sympathisers, junkies, kids, little old ladies, the lot; and they came from every single continent in the world. The funniest ones came from England, where people said, 'Why do you want to come back, Ron? The weather's lousy, the beer is warm and expensive and you can't find a decent curryhouse inside the country – you would be better off staying in Rio!' By far the greatest number, however, commented upon the sentences passed against my dad, and how outrageous it was that he should be sent to prison for such a long time when others, convicted of much more appalling crimes, were freed after only a few years. 'I believe the original sentences passed on the Great Train Robbers were farcical, especially in view of the lenient sentences doled out today for far more serious crimes.' 'How anyone can maintain that a 55-year sentence for a non-violent crime (as far as I know it is neither proven nor especially suspected that your dad hurt the train guard) is just, when the man who killed little Sarah Payne was released after four years for what he did to another little girl, is beyond me.' Others would mention the fact that my father was so ill, it must be costing the British taxpayer a lot of money to keep him in jail, and for what purpose? 'I object to any more of the taxpayers' money being wasted in the persecution of someone. Please let common sense prevail and allow Ronnie Biggs to spend what brief time remains to him with his family.' 'I believe that now is the time for our government to show understanding and compassion and not simply insist on applying the letter of the original sentence, which was set under an entirely different climate from now.' 'I was a prison officer for fifteen years, my feelings are as in the saying "Do the crime and serve the time." But the punishment must fit the crime. After looking back in records on the net I feel that the average sentence for the gang should have been between five and seven years, so I do feel that Ronnie has been dealt with harshly. He is costing us money by being kept inside, he is no danger to society.'

I was going to need some help to handle the volume of e-mails, and I was put in touch with a company called Activ-8 who I asked to host my site while I was getting myself sorted out. They asked me what the appeal was for them, and when I told them that there had been nearly 3 million hits on the site in the previous week alone, they immediately agreed. It was a shame we did not have any sponsors, but I knew that many companies couldn't afford to be associated with Ronnie Biggs, the Great Train Robber, even though they might have liked the notoriety. Also, if I had no morals I could have sold my list of 11,000 addresses to one of several companies who want mailing lists, but I respected everyone's privacy and didn't want to break their trust and expose them to junk mail – I know I hate receiving it. Besides, there's a little thing called the Data Protection Act which prevented me from doing so. We posed a question on the website: 'Should Ronnie Biggs be allowed to come back to England as a free man?' The response was three to one in favour. It is still a powerful website and we get an average of 1,700 hits each week, from all continents.

When I got back to my hotel, everything began to hit me. Because the Sun did not want any other media to be able to reach me, I was a virtual prisoner in my own room. I was registered under a different name – in a nice twist I used the same aliases my father had used when he went on the run years earlier, so I started off as Terence King – the rooms immediately either side of mine were blocked off, as were the ones on the floors directly above and below, and there were security guards patrolling my floor too. I wasn't even allowed to open my window in case photographers caught a glimpse of me. Everyone tried to make me feel comfortable, but I was feeling terribly lonely. I took a shower, ordered some food and then switched on the television. But no matter which channel I turned to, I could not escape the news clips showing my father's arrest when he returned to Britain. I did not want to watch this, so I turned on the radio instead in the hope of finding some music – and the first thing I heard was a news bulletin which also detailed Ronnie Biggs's return and arrest.

There was no escape, and again I was thinking, 'What have I done, what have I done?' I eventually returned to the television and selected the children's cartoon channel. I am not a big cartoon fan, but I had to watch something and anything was better than the news clips devoted to my father. I soon got bored with the cartoons and so I telephoned home to speak to Veronica. But that didn't help too much because she pleaded with me, 'Let me join you, let me and Ingrid come to London to be with you.' I told her there was no way I was bringing her to England where she would be locked in a hotel room for 24 hours a day, it would make her frantic. I didn't want her having to avoid the media like I was, so I told her to enjoy her time in Rio, go to the beach, and not think about it. I told her that if I wanted a glass of Coca-Cola I had to be careful who was bringing it to me, and I didn't want that for her or for our baby, we didn't need the stress. But that only made her get the hump with me, so I told her she would have to give me a couple of months while I sorted everything out.

You can never underestimate the power of the press and it wasn't long before a rival national newspaper found out where I was staying. So, in the middle of the night, I was forced to pack up my things and flee the hotel. I moved instead to the Tower Hotel, which was close to the *Sun*'s headquarters and convenient for Belmarsh just across the river. The hotel knew who I was and put me in a room which was difficult to photograph from the outside, and again the surrounding rooms were blocked off. However, because the *Sun* had been attacked by the Press Complaints Commission for bringing home Ronnie Biggs, they had to break their contract with me, which meant from then on I was on my own and paying for everything myself. With my *Sun* contract broken, I was free to talk to whoever I wanted, and there was no shortage of offers. But I had to be very careful of everybody around me, and that included the people who delivered the room service. I even stood there watching the chamber maids clean my room because I didn't want them going through my things and maybe taking something away to sell to the papers. One morning I had to go out to run a few errands, but I was convinced there would be journalists in the hotel even though nobody knew I was there. Everyone in a suit looked like a journalist – I was in a bad state of paranoia. I put on a jacket with the collar turned up high to cover my face and I donned a baseball cap with the peak pulled down, and I was satisfied I was suitably disguised. As the lift door opened there were two men standing there who I recognised from when we were being hounded in Brazil, but fortunately they were talking and never realised it was me, and so I just got inside and stood in front of them. We stopped at another floor and as I looked up I saw a mate of mine get in the lift who I hadn't seen for two years, but he didn't recognise me either. As the doors closed I whispered to him, 'How are you doing?' He went white when he realised who it was and before he could say anything I said, 'Shush!' and we communicated with our eyes rather than by conversing.

When my contract with the *Sun* ended, Kevin decided it was time to bring in a publicist, so Judy Totton joined our little team. She arranged a press conference for me at my hotel – I figured I would double-bluff the media because they wouldn't expect me to hold it in the hotel in which I was hiding – and I knew this was going to be one of the hardest moments of my life. As a musician I have performed in front of 250,000 people, but the thought of sitting before fifty or so journalists frightened the life out of me. I felt the fact that the *Sun* had got the exclusive story on my father's return meant that these journalists would be out to slaughter me. Other newspapers were already slaughtering my dad and I am sure part of the reason was sour grapes at missing out on one of the biggest stories of the year. They were furious because they couldn't get any information from anyone linked directly to the family. The *Sunday Express* got hold of my mum and put her under contract, but that was all, so I knew the waiting pack would be ready to attack me with questions, such as, 'Was any money made from the *Sun*?' and 'Was a deal cut with the Government?' I knew I could lose it at any moment because of the stress I was under, but we prepared a statement for me to read out at the press conference, and all the time I was feeling very down, especially as it was another ten days before I could next visit my dad. On top of that, the quote I'd just received from the lawyers to take on my dad's case was three times the amount I could afford, but I was so desperate I accepted it anyway, even though I didn't know how I was going to pay for it at that time. So there I was at the press conference, in my blue suit and pink shirt, and I was frightened that the press were going to throw rocks at me. The cameras were flashing and I felt that if I said something wrong they would bring back hanging just for my dad. I had prepared the following statement:

'It is well known that my father escaped from prison and fled the country of his birth 36 years ago. In 1997 the Brazilian Supreme Court rejected the UK's request to extradite my father which guaranteed that he could remain a free man in Brazil for the rest of his life. However, at the age of 71 and fearing that the end of his life is close, he has chosen to voluntarily return to this country. This decision was contrary to my wishes and neither myself nor his family and friends in Brazil could talk him out of it. My father took this decision knowing that he would be arrested and imprisoned. Contrary to some press reports, he has not returned to the UK simply to receive health care. Health care was available in Brazil and my father had many friends and supporters who would certainly have contributed to any such expenses. He has returned to England to end his days in the country that he still thinks of as home. As far as the financial payments are concerned, any payments made by the press are not for my father's direct benefit. As he knows all too well, he has no need of money now. Any payments received by us will be used to contribute to his retrial and legal expenses. He does not wish to be a burden on the British taxpayer. He is also concerned to make some provision for his family, in particular myself and his granddaughter who he may not see again. At a future date his legal team will appeal to the courts and, if necessary, the Home Secretary, to consider whether 28 years imprisonment is, at this stage of his life, an appropriate sentence. My father will, of course, be bound by the decisions of the judges and the Home Secretary. All I ask for, on his behalf, is a fair hearing and a balanced consideration of the true events of the last 35 years of his life. The facts will be placed before the courts in due course. I have nothing further to say at this stage other than I love my dad.

The plan was for me to read the statement then let them ask questions, so I sat down and slowly started to read. But my mind was on my dad and I started shaking; I read a few words and then I lost it; I broke down. I tried to be brave and keep a stiff upper lip but there were a million things going through my head and it was all too much for me, so Judy finished reading the statement for me. There was no way I was going to stay there and let them slaughter me with their questions, so as soon as Judy finished I got up and started to walk away. It was probably one of the most difficult moments of my life. I was very stressed out and we all went back to my room for a meeting, and I put on the television to see how the press conference was going to be portrayed. At that time I had a lot of hatred towards the press because many journalists had suggested I had sold my father, and that hurt. My answer to them is that I am still out there fighting for my dad and I'll never give up on him.

Back in my room we were all sitting there when suddenly we discovered that a joint had been rolled, and Judy went mad. She was right of course, but I had too much on my mind to start giving the guilty party a hard time and I did not want to become part of the argument which broke out. So I screamed at everyone to shut up and I ordered them to leave my room; I needed to be alone and I needed to lie down. Later, my mother came to my room. She had flown over from Switzerland for a couple of days to give me as much moral support as she could. My relationship with my mum had always been very distant, but suddenly, for the first time in 26 years, here she was putting me in her lap. This felt so weird. I was sitting on the floor and she was sitting on the bed behind me massaging my shoulders. It was like, 'Wow, after 26 years I am having some kind of physical contact with my mother.' I still had to keep my distance though, because we live in our separate worlds and always have done, but at least she was giving me as much support as she could, and that was nice.

I was desperate to get out of the hotel, not only to keep my sanity but also because it was running up a big bill and my money was dwindling fast, so I started hunting for a place to live. I found one flat on a council estate which was very nice inside even if the estate wasn't so nice on the outside. I offered to pay the agent up front and told him I did not want anybody to know where I was, but he said, 'If the press want to find you, they will find you.' I knew then I couldn't trust him and I feared that if I rented this flat he would tip off the press where I was just to make a few quid for himself, so I decided against doing business with him. But I didn't have to wait too long because Gio called to say he had found a nice place for me, in Islington, north London. It was a really nice studio in a place for travellers and although the man renting it out knew who I was he was someone we could trust, so I took it, and Johnny and Gio were soon packing my bag for me and helping me to move in. Again I felt very alone in this small room, and I was afraid to go out because I didn't want to blow my cover. I did go for a walk through the grounds of the building, because it was very pleasant with a small pond in the gardens, but every time I heard someone I hid – I was that paranoid. My state of mind was not helped by the fact I became involved in an argument with Bob Starkey, the man who had spent the previous twelve years compiling film footage of my father's life. I had some footage of my own, as I had given a camera to Nick Reynolds and he filmed the whole story of our journey from Brazil, and we were in talks with Channel 5 about making a documentary. I suggested to Starkey that we pool our resources and share the money, and he seemed in favour of the idea. I'd ask for his film, but I found out he was talking to other television producers behind my back and trying to strike a deal without me. The outcome of the row was that Starkey never got release forms signed by my father and the other relevant parties, so his footage became useless and he ended up with no money, when I could have earned him at least £10,000. I was fed up with all the stress from the discussions with Starkey and Channel 5, and so I went to visit Bruce and Nick Reynolds at the Tardis, which is a beautiful cultural centre which raises money for the Sunshine Orphanage in Egypt. Nick is friends with the owner, George. I was sitting there chatting to them when Kevin rang me. He said, 'Mike, I just had a call from the prison governor, he wants to talk to you immediately.' I asked him what it was all about, but he just said, 'He won't tell me, you had better call him.' I rang the prison and the duty governor was very nice to me. He told me they thought my father had suffered another stroke, which was all I needed at that time. I had been in England for a month, I was trying to settle in and get my life in order, I had pressure from Veronica who wanted to join me, there was the trouble with Starkey holding up the documentary, and now my father had taken a turn for the worse. I had few genuine friends either, and ironically Kevin was inundated with calls from people who were supposedly old friends and wanted to get in touch with me. But many of these were the same people who'd turned their backs when I needed their help some months earlier, so there was no way I was going to return their calls when they obviously wanted to jump on the bandwagon now. However, I also knew there were still some genuine friends ringing Kevin who cared about me and wanted to know what was going on, but I did not want to speak to them all and have to repeat my story over and over again. If I snubbed them, I didn't mean anything personal and I hope they understand.

I didn't know what I was going to do, but when that call came in I needed to get to the hospital right away. My father had been transferred from Belmarsh to the Queen Elizabeth Hospital in Woolwich after the attack, and it was going to cost me £30 to 40 in a taxi from north London to south London. I thought my dad was probably dying, and I needed to get there fast, but I didn't know public transport very well, so a taxi was my only option. I hailed half a dozen cabs, but none of them were prepared to go south of the river! Eventually, I flagged down a cabbie and when he also refused to take me I said, 'I'll tell you what, if you take me there now I'll give you £100.' He said, 'Are you serious?' so I said, 'Look, I am fucking Ronnie Biggs's son, my dad is dying in hospital, will you stop wasting my time and take me!' I showed him the money and he told me to jump in, and I was heading to see my dad. When I arrived at the hospital Kevin was waiting at the door for me and the press were everywhere. My father had not been booked in as Ronnie Biggs, and I thought the choice of name chosen for him – Mr Sweeney – was certainly an interesting one. Perhaps they had the Flying Squad keeping an eye on him again!

When I found the room in which they were holding my dad, once again I couldn't believe what I saw. My father was lying in bed, with a drip attached to one hand – and his other hand was cuffed to a prison officer. My father was looking confused because in total there were six prison guards and four police officers in this little room: ten people to guard one frail old man who had just had another stroke.

In front of all of them I just broke down, and I kept asking, 'Why?' The officer who was handcuffed to my father was a guy in his late fifties and I could see the look of shame on his face. He could not look me in the eye, but he did say, 'Michael, I am sorry, these orders came from way above – I am so sorry.' There then followed a ridiculous scene as they took my father for a brain scan. Two of the officers went with him, one chained to my dad and the other standing beside him. The hospital staff told the officers they would have to leave all their metal – including the handcuffs – outside the room as it would interfere with the scanning machine. The officers tried to argue with the staff, so I stepped in to try and resolve things. I said, 'Come on guys, they are going to put him inside a machine, he is not about to go anywhere; there are no windows in here, you will not be breaking any regulations, he can't escape. Just call another officer in, leave the handcuffs, keys and whistles with him and then stand in the room. Let's try and be reasonable.' Then they relented and the brain scan went ahead, which confirmed my father had suffered another minor stroke. I went outside and faced the press, and told them about the ten guards. It went out live on television, and within ten minutes the Home Office phoned the hospital and told the guards to remove the handcuffs, because they were getting bad publicity; the press had started calling them to ask if it was necessary to have ten people guarding a sick old man. The other point in all of this was that it was wasting taxpayers' money. I actually spoke to the guards and found out how much they were being paid. The prison officers were getting £58 an hour and the police officers were getting £63 an hour. My father was being guarded 24-hours a day, and when I did the maths it worked out as costing a staggering £14,400 a day – and that was before the hospital costs were taken into account. I did not want such expensive treatment for my father. I would gladly have footed every bill, if only they would have allowed him to come and stay with me in my flat, so that I could look after him myself. I think the treatment was way over the top. After I complained to the press and they contacted the Home Office the guard was cut down to four people, but that still worked out at nearly £6,000 a day, and my father was in hospital for a week. My father returned to Belmarsh but was in such poor health that the prison called me to say I could visit him twice a week on compassionate grounds, so that made a nice difference for me.

I was feeling lonely and needed cheering up so Max Carlish, one of the producers from Channel 5 who had previously visited my father in Brazil on his seventieth birthday, threw a party for me. There I met a man who said he had mixed feelings about my dad but had a lot of sympathy for me. He wanted to help out, and he owned some property in the City of London area, which he was prepared to let me rent for a very special deal. He showed me a great flat, although it was painted pink, which I didn't really mind, and that became my new home. It was just what I needed because I had used the money I had to settle my debts in Brazil, and what I had left was rapidly running out. The flat was partly furnished, so Gio took me to the local Argos store where we could buy the cheapest electrical goods and pots and pans. I knew this would be only a temporary home for me, especially as the Home Office could kick me out at any time. We also went to a second-hand shop for some office furniture, so that I could set up my computers to run the website. Everything was done on a budget, apart from the two things I value most in my life, which are my laptop and my acoustic guitar. This was another reason I knew my father had sent Gio to look after me – he knew where to find the cheapest bed and all the other essentials. I was on the up, and another boost was just around the corner because I had arranged for Veronica and Ingrid to come for a visit. I had been in England for nearly three months and had endured a lot of problems, so I was desperate to see my family, and when they arrived it was like being in paradise. My daughter was running around shouting, 'Dad-dy, Dad-dy,' and my wife was all over me. What more could a man want? Both of them were so happy that the three of us were reunited, I was overwhelmed. There was another visitor too, my next-door neighbour from Santa Theresa, called Jimmy, who had been working with me on the website since my father had suffered his second stroke. I gave him a job again working on the website with us and was able to catch up on life back in Rio. The website was doing well because we were visiting Internet chat rooms, talking about Ronnie Biggs and pulling people into our campaign for his freedom.

The next thing which happened to break the peace was that I was called by the immigration office to be told it was time for my interview. I decided to answer every question they threw at me with as much honesty and dignity as possible, but that proved to be a mistake, and I think I would have been better off lying to them. The first thing they told me was they had made a mistake by giving me the right to seek employment, and that the officer who had greeted me at the airfield had got it wrong. I couldn't believe it. Picture the scene: my father flies back into Britain, there are 110 police officers to greet us on the tarmac, the Flying Squad are ready to storm the plane, they send one of the top immigration officers to handle the paperwork – and he gets it wrong. A likely story. After my interview they told me they would be in touch soon, and sure enough I received a call just 24 hours later asking me to go back for another interview. By now, Veronica and Ingrid were in the country and so I was grilled by the immigration authorities as to why my wife and daughter were here, and what our plans were. I think they feared I would try to settle here, but that was not on my agenda, and I tried to assure them that Veronica was just here to visit my father and me, and that she had a return ticket booked to Rio. I didn't want my daughter raised in Britain: she goes to the beach three times a week and has a tropical lifestyle, and I didn't want her to swap that for a life in the grey weather of England. Also, Veronica was studying at college and did not want to give that up. I think the mistake I made was to tell them I wanted to stay in the country and fight for my father's liberty or reduction of sentence, and that I wanted to work so that I could maintain myself. I wasn't interested in claiming any benefits. But they denied my application, so I decided to appeal on the grounds that my human rights were being breached. While this interview was going on, Veronica was waiting at London Bridge for me because we were going to visit my father. This would have been the first time she had seen him since he left Brazil and she was looking forward to it very much. But I was so stunned when I left the interview that I just stood there smoking a cigarette, my first since giving up a couple of months earlier. Then Veronica rang my mobile phone and told me to hurry up or we would miss the visit, but I told her to go home and forget about it because I had just been given the news that I couldn't stay in the country. I was depressed, but there was more serious news just around the corner.

We rebooked our prison visit for a couple of days later and when we turned up to see my dad I could see there was something wrong. When I asked him he wrote, 'I am shitting blood.' I then asked him what the doctors had said about that, but he told me they didn't take any notice of him, so I called someone to tell them what was happening and they promised to investigate. It took them a whole week before they discovered he had lost two pints of blood, and he was rushed into hospital again so that he could be given a blood transfusion. I was heavily involved in my battle with the immigration authorities so Veronica and Ingrid visited my father every day instead. After the problems they had in Brazil it was great to see Veronica by his side, and she wanted to make sure that all their differences were behind them; she did not want any bitterness. She loved my father and I knew he regarded her as a daughter before he had his stroke and his mind started playing him up. In the good old days I would come home from work and the two of them would be sitting there with a glass of wine each, chatting about anything and everything. So when it was time for Veronica to go back to Brazil she was heartbroken, because we didn't know when we would next see each other. She actually left on my birthday. I was also still worried about my financial position, because I was not allowed to work in the UK. I could have earned money back at home: I'd been made a big-money offer from a television production company who wanted me to fly back to Brazil and make a documentary on Brazilian gangsters and warlords. I made a few phone calls and set everything up because I had good contacts from the music industry – I knew musicians who came from poor backgrounds and whose brothers had connections with the drug world as a result. I was told that Michael Biggs could have the freedom to film whatever he wanted in the slums, and they would give me protection and anything else I needed. But I knew that if I left Britain they would not let me back in, so eventually I had to turn it down.

Back in Santa Theresa, Veronica was living in the house, but the spirit had gone from it without my father there. There was a sad atmosphere there and so I decided it was time to retire Rosa, the woman who had worked for my father since I was five, and who had helped him raise me and been like a mother to me in many ways. An added problem was that the neighbourhood had suddenly become violent and dangerous; there were reports of rapes and murders. My neighbour Jim had told me how he'd gone out one night to have a beer, and tripped over a body which had been shot moments earlier, as the blood was still trickling from the wound. Needless to say, he abandoned the idea of having a beer and rushed back indoors. I was worried about Veronica and Ingrid living alone. Matters were not helped by the fact that there were grossly exaggerated reports in the local press of how much money I was supposed to be making from my father's return to Britain, which attracted unwanted attention, and I knew Veronica was freaking out. There was barbed wire and video surveillance cameras around the house and she had Blitz, our Rottweiler, but the dog could not defend the two of them against bullets. Veronica loved Santa Theresa when I was there and hated it when I wasn't. She was afraid to go out and was having things delivered to the house, but even then she was frightened to walk to the gates of the house in the dark to collect them. I wanted her to feel secure so told her to get out and book into a hotel temporarily while she looked for somewhere else to live. With the house empty, my dog Blitz was not being properly cared for, so I asked a friend of mine to move into the house and keep an eye on things; he asked if he could take his mother, and that suited me because I knew she would stop him from throwing any wild parties. With Veronica living in a reasonably expensive hotel, I was again running out of money fast. Judy my publicist was keen to protect my image and turned down a lot of interview offers, but that meant it cost me more money, and all I had was the money coming in from Channel 5 for the documentary.

It usually takes about six months before you are given a ruling on a human rights appeal but, amazingly, in my case I heard it had been denied within three weeks; so I decided to appeal. To then receive a hearing date can take another year but, again, I was given a date some four or five months earlier than could normally be expected. I was not unhappy, though, because the faster it was sorted out, the faster I could start earning money for myself legally. I did not want benefits, just the right to stay in the country on humanitarian grounds and be allowed to work. Instead, the Government wanted to bleed me dry until I could not afford to stay here any more, but they didn't realise that they were dealing with a tough cookie. This country was supposed to be the place where human rights started, the belly button of the universe, and I felt that terrorists and freeloaders posing as asylum seekers were getting a better deal than me, but I was not going to give up my fight.

10. LIFE GOES ON

A few months after my father had returned to England, the Ronnie Biggs story was becoming less interesting to the newspapers, so I decided to lie low for a while and wait until interest picked up again. The only approaches I made to the media happened on my birthday, when I held a press conference to say that I felt the way my father was being treated was appalling. I had found out that, on one occasion when he had to be taken to hospital, the prison didn't even bother to let me know; I also learned, at the same time, that he hadn't been seen for three months in Belmarsh by the prison doctor. A very kind speech therapist discovered my father's medical files and noticed that nobody had seen him. She went to the prison off her own back to see him and they told her she couldn't because she hadn't filled in the relevant forms. But she threatened them by saying that unless she was allowed in, she would tell me she had been barred from seeing my father, and they did not need the bad publicity, so they let her see him. Then one day she rang me to say she had just seen my father in one of the rooms in the hospital. He had been there for 24 hours and nobody had contacted me. The prison told our lawyers that they don't usually contact the family if a prisoner goes to hospital unless it is an unusual situation. I blew my top with one of the governors, because they knew full well that ours was an unusual situation. My father had suffered three strokes by now and I was his only family, and they didn't have the decency to call me. I hope the people in charge are embarrassed by this.

Not long after that episode I received a telephone call from the *Daily Mail*, saying they had something very interesting which they wanted to show me before it was published. I am always very careful in situations like this, so I arranged to meet the reporter in a pub but then changed the venue at the last minute in case he had arranged for people to be there watching us. He showed me a picture of my father asleep in his cell which someone had sent to them, and it was pretty bad as it showed my father in squalid conditions, with a tube coming out of his nose. This was a very big breach of security as far as the prison was concerned. They knew I had nothing to do with the picture, because it had been taken at night, but from that day on I was barred from seeing my father in the health-care wing and had instead to visit him in the main visiting room. But they were still trying to hide my dad from the other prisoners, because he had a feeding tube coming out of his nose, and this made it clear that he wasn't well enough to stay in prison (besides making him look a bit of a freak), so they put us on a special watch table, called the A1 table. That is the table closest to the prison guards, and the one which has two surveillance cameras focused on it at all times. It became a standard joke, and when I got to the booking-in table and looked for my dad's name I would just say 'A1'.

Belmarsh is a prison where a lot of 'colourful characters' pass through. Ronnie Biggs was regarded as the biggest celebrity in the prison, but he was joined at one point by another high-profile 'criminal' in the shape of Lord Jeffrey Archer. I think Archer was quite excited when he knew my dad was already in Belmarsh and not long after he arrived there he went up to meet my dad and shake his hand. My dad wrote down, 'Nice to meet you, Lord Archer,' and Archer hurriedly told him, 'Please don't call me Lord, especially not in here. You can call me Jeffrey.' I wouldn't be surprised if the story of their meeting turns up in one of Archer's future novels, or that he has a character in one of them based on the legendary Ronnie Biggs. My father and Archer actually met in the hospital wing of Belmarsh while Archer was put on suicide watch. That does not mean that the authorities thought Archer was going to commit suicide. What happens is that every time a new inmate is admitted to Belmarsh, they spend some time in the hospital wing – where my father is based permanently – on suicide watch regardless of whether or not they are suicidal; it is just a standard procedure. Archer was then put in the cell next door to my father, until one of the lunatics torched his cell and they had to move him. My dad's cell is special – it is the only one with an electrical socket in it, so that he can use a feeding machine. Therefore they cannot keep switching him from cell to cell, otherwise they would have to call an electrician every time.

Archer did not stay in Belmarsh for too long; he was transferred to an open prison because of who he is, but if my dad had his full speech then I am sure Archer would have done everything in his power to have spent more time with him, because they would have made good intellectual partners for each other. The thing which attached my father and Bruce Reynolds to each other all those years ago was the fact they wanted to educate themselves while they were doing time. They didn't want just to lift weights. While most of the cons went to the gym to become bigger and stronger, my dad and Bruce went to the library to learn. It must be very hard for my old man as such an educated man not to hold intelligent conversations. I know my father would have turned to Archer and said, 'So you have read Sartre, have you? Well so fucking have I. You understand Shakespeare? You just tell me a line of Shakespeare and I'll tell you which sonnet it is from; and if you are not careful I will tell you what page it is on.' I know this because my father studied Shakespeare really hard. He also has a fantastic botanical knowledge, so David Bellamy eat your heart out! He knows the names of plants, how to plant them, how to cut them, anything. He taught himself so much over the years.

Although Belmarsh holds people who have committed serious crimes, if you are in the hospital wing then you are either sick or you are a Samaritan. The Samaritans are prisoners who have shown compassion and they help to look after other prisoners. They also have extra privileges such as more cigarettes or telephone calls. There have been lots of different Samaritans who have helped care for my old man, and a lot of them feel very sorry for him. If my dad drops something on his trousers he cannot clean it himself, so they wash his clothes for him and iron them. They also read letters to him because his eyes are not good. But there is a big element of kudos attached to this because it means a lot in the underworld society for criminals to say they did time with someone as notorious as Ronnie Biggs. I have lost count of the number of people who have come up to me over the years and said, 'Michael, I knew your dad on the inside, I met him before he did the train job.' Well my dad must have been one hell of a popular guy, because he did only ten years inside. How many people can you meet in that time? But I don't argue with anyone because if they are happy to say they did time with my dad then that is OK with me.

My dad, because of his character, usually wins the sympathy of people. But there was one female senior officer working at the prison whose attitude was, 'We are not going to have any heroes in here,' and she behaved like a real bitch towards him. She really got on his case, and said he could have only a certain number of CDs, he could receive only a certain number of letters, and things like that. But my dad started making jokes about her to other inmates. He would write things down such as, 'Doesn't she look sexy today in those baggy jeans,' or, 'Don't you just love the way she has done her hair and nails today,' and this really made other people laugh. The old man is great for giving people nicknames; he knows how to spot something in someone's character and come up with a funny name. For example, his first nurse in prison was black and had a distinctive hairstyle, so he named her 'Whoopi' after the American actress Whoopi Goldberg. The name stuck, and everybody calls her Whoopi now. Eventually, the hard-nosed officer got to know my dad and realised he was just a weak old man, and she developed a real soft spot for him and is crazy about him. She even joked with him to let her be a bridesmaid at his wedding. He gets on well with a lot of the screws because he has such a good memory. If they tell him the name of their children he will remember, and then say to them, 'How is little Johnny? You told me he had a birthday coming up, let me give you an autograph to give him as a present,' and they respect that. So even though prisoners are allowed only eleven CDs each, my dad has a few more because he can't read books. Instead he sits there listening to his jazz and Brazilian music, Bossa Nova. My father is a big jazz enthusiast.

My immigration appeal hearing under the Human Rights Act was heard in November 2001 and I was bullied by the prosecutor, who asked me why I wanted to remain in England. When I told him I wanted to be with my father, he asked why I couldn't leave and come back as a tourist. I said, 'I know that if I leave Britain I will be refused re-entry.' He said, 'But we have never said that,' and I replied, 'Nor have you given me any guarantees that I will be allowed back in, and without them I am not leaving.' He thought he was smart because then he asked me why I hadn't contacted the British authorities in Rio before we came to Britain to sort all this out. So I said to him, 'Look sir, you work for the Home Office, so I thought you would know there has been an order in place for more than twenty years that nobody at the embassy in Brazil should have any contact with my family whatsoever. If the ambassador or consul are having dinner at a restaurant and my father walks in, they have to pay their bill and walk out. And now you are telling me I should have contacted them?' He quickly changed the subject. He grilled me about the number of times I had been to see my father, and suggested it wasn't very many for someone who was here to be close to their father. However, he manipulated the figures in two ways. First of all, he did not allow for the fact that in the early days I was allowed to see my father only on a fortnightly basis. Then secondly, he had counted only the prison visits and had ignored the visits I had made to my father when he was in hospital, because then I had been allowed to see him on a daily basis. He also pointed out the fact that a couple of friends had visited dad, and suggested he didn't really need my visits as he could get moral support from these friends. We got into a verbal fight, and we had to be separated by the adjudicator. This all happened on a Friday, and these cases usually take four to six weeks before a decision arrives in the post, but because my situation was high profile, the adjudicator said there would be a decision the following Monday! Once again, because I was Michael Biggs, I was being fast-tracked, which was harsh on people who were waiting weeks for a decision. Another interesting aspect was that I was actually encouraged to use a loophole, whereby I was advised after six months to leave the country for a day, then come back in for an extra six months as a tourist. But I knew they just wanted an excuse to get me out of Britain so they could refuse my re-entry, because they gave me no guarantees.

The decision came on the Monday, and I was denied a visa to remain in Britain. The reason given was that it would cause a disturbance. As soon as I heard that, I had an image going through my mind of lots of cars being overturned and set on fire, and people looting shops, and gangs rioting – all because Michael Biggs got a visa to stay in the country. Gee, I didn't know I had that much power – maybe I should have been a politician. It was just an excuse because they didn't want me in the country. I would have preferred the truth, rather than an excuse, which I felt made the authorities look stupid. So I immediately lodged an appeal. I then had to go to the hospital in south-east London to tell my father I had lost. He was back in hospital because he had ulcers in his stomach and had again been losing blood, and he was about to have an operation. As well as that bad news, we heard that the CCRC, the Criminal Cases Review Commission, were not going to refer my father's case to the Court of Appeal, because they claimed there was insufficient evidence. Our argument was that if Buster Edwards got fifteen years and he was one of the train robbery gang's leaders, then why did my dad, who was just a tea boy in comparison, get 55 years – 25 for robbery and 30 for conspiracy. So I had to break the double bad news to my father. I was worried about how he would take the news while he was getting ready for a stomach operation. I decided to play a game, so I walked into his hospital room smiling and said, 'Dad, we've lost.' He wrote down, 'Then why are you looking so fucking happy?' I replied that I had been expecting to lose. He wasn't convinced, but he told me to continue fighting. I then received a bollocking from the hospital staff because Uri Geller had visited my dad and I hadn't pre-warned them. It had created a bit of a media circus, which they were unhappy about, and they made me promise to warn them next time any high-profile visitors were due. While I was at the hospital, I found out that the Home Office had been sending their own doctors there to look at my dad, because they did not trust the NHS doctors. I overheard an argument in the corridor outside my dad's room between someone from the Home Office and one of the doctors. My father had been in the hospital for thirty days and they wanted him sent back to prison. The doctors later admitted to me privately that they were under pressure to send him back, but were resisting the Home Office because they felt my father was too sick to go back to that prison hospital wing. But once my father had the operation, he did have to go back to Belmarsh.

By this time it had been four months since I had seen Veronica and Ingrid, and they were again missing me and needed to see me. I couldn't return to Brazil, so I had to find the money to fly them over to London to see me instead. I think the British government were hoping to bleed me dry by denying me the right to work, in the hope that I would give up and return to Brazil, but I was continuing the fight. Every time the press called the Home Office they said they had no intention of removing Michael Biggs. But then again, they had no intention of granting Michael Biggs a visa, not that they would admit that. I didn't realise at the time, but they would not even let me do voluntary work, and after I made a personal appearance at a fundraising event for the Stroke Institute during Stroke Awareness Week, I got told off by the Home Office, although they let that one slip by. There was a financial light at the end of the tunnel because of this book coming out, but even that was tough for me because I had to write about my dad's life, and about his illness, and about some of the painful things in my life. But it was also my chance to tell some funny stories about my life, set the record straight and put my side of the story about how the British government was treating me, and I wanted to do that. At least I would not get into trouble with the Home Office, as they told me I could write a book, make a documentary or record an album.

Veronica and Ingrid were arriving in England so I went to the airport to meet them. I saw all these Brazilians coming into the arrivals hall, but no sign of my wife and daughter, and the alarm bells started ringing in my head. I thought, 'The Home Office has held them, what are they going to do to them?' I waited for an hour and forty minutes and still nothing, so I rang the Home Office, and they confirmed Veronica and Ingrid were being detained while they were making inquiries. I said to the woman on the other end of the telephone, 'You are not making inquiries, you are holding my daughter because she is Ronnie Biggs's granddaughter, and you are holding my wife because she is Ronnie Biggs's daughter-in-law. You have no reason to do this. My wife has told you why she is here and where she is going to be staying.' The woman told me they still had to make a few inquiries, but that an immigration officer would come out to see me. The immigration officer said they were not doing anything wrong, and they were going to be letting them out within fifteen minutes. But half an hour later there was still no sign of them, so I started to call the press. Before long, both the *News of the World* and ITN had reporters, photographers and camera crew on standby, ready to come to the airport if necessary. I then spoke to the woman in immigration and asked if they would send someone out to face the media. She said that was not necessary, and that my wife and daughter would be out in ten minutes. But fifteen minutes later, I was still waiting, and I was just about to call my lawyers, when suddenly the doors opened and out walked Veronica, looking totally destroyed, with Ingrid asleep in her arms. Veronica had been held for four hours in total, and she just burst into tears. The authorities had not even offered them a glass of water to drink or a chair to sit in – nothing. I gave Ingrid a kiss and said, 'Daddy's here.' She half woke up and was thrilled to see me, and Veronica just sat on a luggage trolley and broke down, asking why they had done that to her. She told me how they had searched all of Ingrid's toys, and copied the telephone numbers of her friends which Veronica had written in her diary. I called off the press and took my wife and daughter home. I wrote to the Home Office asking why they'd done it, but they never gave me the answers.

It was during Veronica's stay that I received a call from the parole board. This came about after Gio found out via the Internet that every prisoner has the right to apply to the prison governor or the Home Secretary for an early release on compassionate grounds, if they are in ill health. So the call came in from a parole officer who told me they needed to carry out a home inspection of the place where I lived, so I should expect a visit within the next three hours. Once again, it had slipped somebody's mind to do the decent thing and give me a few days' notice, but they had to visit me then because a parole hearing was scheduled to take place 48 hours later. It was all being done on the British government's terms, and our solicitors were refused permission to attend the parole hearing. Shortly after the board met, I received a letter from the Home Secretary, David Blunkett, saying he did not think my father should be let out of prison on compassionate grounds because he can walk two-hundred yards unaided. But that was bollocks: my father couldn't go fifty yards without someone by his side because he could lose his balance at any moment. To be honest, I had not got my hopes up about this in the first place, because I didn't expect them to be compassionate, and I think they were simply going through the motions. They said my father would have to carry on serving his time, but they were ready to reconsider if his health deteriorated. That decision was followed by a final letter from the CCRC, who said they were not ready to refer my father's case to the Court of Appeal, because they felt the 55-year sentence imposed on him was fair. I think they feared that if they gave my dad a fairer sentence for the crime, he would probably get ten years for robbery and seven years for conspiracy, which means he would have to serve ten years. Out of that ten, a third would be knocked off automatically, leaving him with six years and nine months to do. My Dad did 22 months before he escaped from Wandsworth, and with the time served since returning to Britain, he would be eligible for parole in May 2002. Our next step was to go for a judicial review. I also decided to write an open letter to Mr Blunkett, and after much deliberation I came up with the following:

Dear Mr Blunkett,

What can the British government possibly gain from allowing my father, Ronald Biggs, to die in prison? I've been fighting for justice for my father ever since his voluntary return to England. I am making this personal plea to you as all avenues have been exhausted. You are my final hope.

To rule that my father should see out the remainder of his sentence is the easy option. To question the severity of the original sentence and to conclude that he does not deserve to spend his remaining days behind bars is a far more difficult option. However, I pray that you will find the courage and the compassion to do just that, as I have lost all faith in the British justice system.

My father instilled in me a great British resolve, to fight for what I truly believe in. Mr Blunkett, I am fighting for my father's life. I thank God that I am not alone in my struggle, and the overwhelming support I've received has given me the strength and the belief that the voice of the people is very powerful.

The gang of sixteen who carried out 'The Great Train Robbery' was made up of two different London gangs. My father was a member of neither. He simply knew a train driver, and was propositioned to take part. Out of greed, he foolishly accepted the offer. He never stepped foot on the train, in fact his status was such that he was ordered to sit next to the getaway driver. In contrast, the getaway driver in the recent Dome case received five years for his involvement in the attempted robbery. My father received concurrent sentences of 30 years for robbery and 25 years for conspiracy. A shocking total of 55 years. Mr Blunkett, does that fit the crime? Sadly, The Criminal Cases Review Commission recently decided that it did. If this is British justice, then frankly, I am appalled.

Had he received a fair sentence, my father always said that he would have accepted it and served his time. He was absolutely devastated by the crushing sentence. At a time when there was no parole system, that meant a minimum of twenty years in prison. Faced with the prospect of losing his family and his life, he was offered the opportunity to escape and took it.

In 1970, my father arrived in Brazil with only $200 to his name and his only thought was of building a new life for himself. He had no intention of going back into a life of crime, and just wanted to put the past behind him and make an honest go of it. In 1974, when the Brazilian authorities realised my father was wanted by the British police, they imposed their own punishment; he was placed on bail, which required him to sign on twice weekly at a police station, imposed a 10 p.m. curfew and was prevented from working or marrying. He adhered to this for 32 years, notwithstanding the mental torture of having to live under the constant threat of extradition. He was once brutally kidnapped. It was never my father's intention to become known as 'The Great Train Robber,' that was of the British media's making. He was forced to live off his wits. It was a question of survival.

My father is a reformed man. A law-abiding citizen for 38 years, he didn't want to die a fugitive in a foreign country. He is British and wanted to come home. This took a great deal of courage and as much as he expected to be punished, he did not expect to be treated so inhumanely. Where is the British sense of fair play that my father always told me about? Perhaps times have changed and it is a thing of the past.

When I was old enough to understand, my father explained to me that he had made a terrible mistake, one that he deeply regretted. He left me in no doubt that crime does not pay. In my mother's absence, he was always there for me, single-handedly raising me, giving me the correct values and morals, teaching me right from wrong. It is now my duty as his proud son to put the record straight.

His current medical condition is extremely poor. My father has had three strokes and has suffered two epileptic seizures. He is being fed through a tube that has been inserted into his stomach. He suffers from stomach ulcers, gastrointestinal haemorrhaging, is unable to speak, eat, swallow or drink. He is a very sick man, and requires specialist medical treatment currently not on offer to him in Belmarsh.

I find it completely inconsistent with your proposed prison reforms, to keep my father incarcerated. You state that public protection is your priority, yet keep my father imprisoned. If released, do you believe that he would re-offend? That he would be a menace and a danger to the public? It costs the taxpayer in excess of £2,000 per week to hold my father in top security Belmarsh and, as you yourself have stated, prison is an expensive way of denying people liberty. Surely it would make more sense to release him under licence into my care, placing less of a strain on the public purse and freeing up space in your overcrowded prisons.

We are now in the 21st century. The powers that be seem intent on punishing a man for his bit-part role in the theft of money. Given the fact that this crime took place almost forty years ago, the retribution, cruelty and inhumanity demonstrated by the British authorities has no place in a civilised society. It is time to move on.

Has my father become a trophy for the British government? A political prisoner of the 21st century? He is a good, decent man and does not deserve to be turned into a political scapegoat. Politics should not be allowed to get in the way of justice.

My father is not a murderer, a terrorist, a paedophile or a rapist. He was once a small time thief who, on the day of his 33rd birthday, made the costliest mistake of his life. He is now an extremely frail 72-year-old man and has been punished enough.

In the name of humanity, grant my father the dignity and the right to see out his remaining days as a free man.

Michael Biggs

With the British government playing silly buggers and refusing to give me a visa for a year, which would allow me at least to work and support myself, I had to fall back on a last resort. Asylum seekers come into Britain and receive housing benefit, food vouchers and all sorts, without being properly checked out, and the Government allows itself to be pissed on. But because I am Ronnie Biggs's son, I get different treatment. My denial when I appealed on the grounds of human rights was the fastest refusal in history. People wait for two years for a result and mine came in three months. Why?

I am not trying to get back at the British public, but I have been driven to pursue a full British passport by a few arseholes in suits who think they can treat me how they want. I didn't ask for anything unreasonable, just a temporary visa so I could remain here legally to care for and support my father, a frail and decent old man. I only wanted to stay for a year, and then a further year if the matter wasn't resolved, but they didn't want to be humane and they denied me the right to work for eleven months of my life, which meant I drained all my resources and couldn't properly support my family back home in Brazil. As it happened, my father – who over the years has proposed to her three times – finally married my mother in Belmarsh prison on 10 July 2002. Britain boasts about how fair it is on human rights, but I have not found that to be the case. Had I not been granted a passport, I would have taken the Government to the European Court of Human Rights, and I know I would have won the right to stay here. So I feel bitter towards the British government. It seems that it is OK for them to let a mad fundamentalist into the country and then turn a blind eye while they recruit more terrorists, but they cannot allow someone to stay here to care for his sick father. It hurts me to think that by keeping me here under restrictions, the British government has deprived me of an important year in the life of my daughter. I have not seen her develop into a lively and happy two-year-old. I left Brazil when she could not yet talk, and now she can chatter away merrily, as I find out when I speak to her via the Internet or on the telephone. She is changing so much and I am missing a formative period in her life. They are punishing my father, making him serve his thirty years, and also being hard on my family. Hopefully our lives will become settled again one day and we can pick ourselves up again and even think about having more children.

I have made so much in my life, and I have also lost so much. My main concern now is that my daughter Ingrid has some kind of future. I don't give a fuck about myself, as long as I can pay my bills. I want to teach my daughter everything my dad has taught me. I may be only 27 but I have experienced a lot and I want to share those experiences with her and tell her about Mount Fuji, or the Andes, or the Gulf of Mexico, or singing to huge crowds and flying in balloons – things a regular parent cannot tell their children. Once my dad has departed, as far as I am concerned I can go to a farm somewhere in Brazil and plant onions for the rest of my life. There is nothing out there I haven't seen: I have jammed with the Stones, I have travelled the world and visited a variety of places, from Disneyland to whorehouses; I have had the limousines and dined in the fancy restaurants, and at the other end of the scale I have tasted what it is like not to have a single penny in my pocket. It is hard to impress me nowadays; not many things can shock me. I have seen people being shot in front of me, and all kinds of shit in my life. I have no great ambitions to fulfil. At least I have my music. I have been invited by the So Solid Crew to play guitar on some of the tracks of their new album, and that has been a nice experience. Ronnie Biggs recorded with the Sex Pistols and Michael has recorded with the modern-day equivalent. I am also working on my own album and I hope that is a success. Of course I would like to be on-stage again in front of thousands of people, with my own band, earning pots of money, but I have had that before and so I will not be frustrated if it never happens again. I would not like to be in the pop world in the same way as I was when I was a young child. That is not me any more, and I don't mind if I end up playing in pubs for the rest of my life. I am proud and delighted that Veronica has agreed to marry me, and so we are going to be married in summer 2002, in England. I am laid back about the future of Michael Biggs. But one thing I do know is that I shall always remain deeply proud to be the son of the legendary Great Train Robber, Ronnie Biggs.

INDEX